THE HOLINESS OF

WOMANHOOD

MARY KLOSKA

En Route Books and Media, LLC
St. Louis, MO

Make the time

En Route Books and Media, LLC
5705 Rhodes Avenue
St. Louis, MO 63109

Cover credit: Mary Kloska (image) and TJ Burdick (design)

Library of Congress Control Number: 2020943272

ISBN-13: 978-1-952464-23-2

"The more a woman is holy,
the more she becomes a woman."[1]

The Maria Bambina

This book is consecrated to Our Lady,
our Littlest and Dearest and Holiest Mother.
She is the Mystic Rose, the Desert Rose,
that blooms forth in all kinds of weather.
She is truly God's Masterpiece of Femininity.

---

[1] Sheen, Fulton J. *The World's First Love, Mary the Mother of God* (San Francisco: Ignatius Press, 1952), p. 83.

Contents

To the Reader at the Beginning…

Before the reader begins this book, I ask her to take a few moments of silence to settle her heart before God. In this time, we ask the Father, Jesus, and the Holy Spirit, Who are the only Ones with keys to our hearts, to come and open them before Him. We ask Them to open our eyes, to open our ears, to open our hearts to be a resting place for Their work. More than anything else, this is a retreat—a time when we withdraw from our normal activities in the world to commune with God, to open our lives before Him, and to allow Him to touch us deep within, cleaning our wounds, and forming us new to be His Own.

Hail Mary, full of Grace,
The Lord is with Thee.
Blessed art thou among women
And blessed is the fruit of thy womb, Jesus.
Holy Mary, Mother of God,
Pray for us sinners
Now and at the hour of our death.
Amen.
Come Holy Spirit!
Come by the means of the powerful intercession
Of the Immaculate Heart of Mary,
Your most beloved spouse.
Amen.

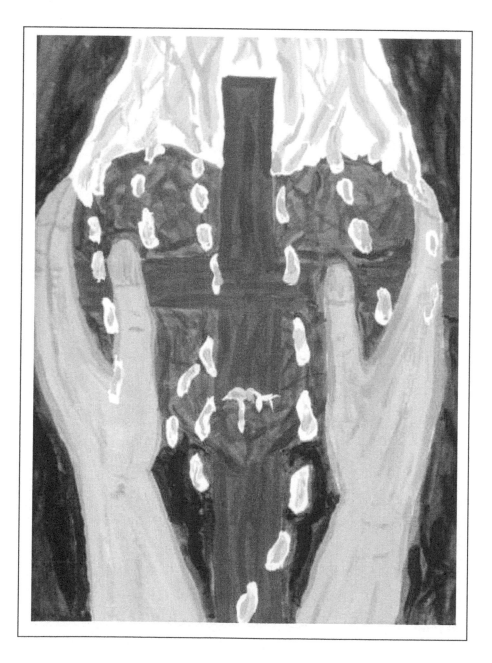

This book is a gift of a retreat for women—a time when a woman leaves the ordinary actions of her life to enter in a special way into the presence of God so that He can draw her closer to Himself. This book contains teachings, and yet the greatest Teacher will be God Himself Who responds to each woman's prayer asking for Him to be with her in this special time.

The time set apart for this retreat is a consecrated time. When one has an ordinary cup, it can be used for one's normal, everyday life. But when it is consecrated for Mass (as a chalice), it is put aside for a special purpose, a holy purpose. And so I ask for each woman to take this time when she is reading this book and to set it aside in a consecrated way so that God can use it for a holy purpose. As each woman experiences this retreat, the Holy Spirit is with her, for she has asked Him to be. And so He Himself will come to transform her by His very presence with her. God Himself will speak to each woman's heart, because by embarking on this retreat she is giving Him her life saying, '*I want to learn more about who You created me to be.*' And so I encourage each woman to watch her life—everything that happens while she is reading this retreat—because in a certain way God will be opening up things to her that I could never speak to her.

I cannot speak to each woman's individual heart all the time because each woman is so very different. I must speak in generalities, and often in life there are exceptions to such generalities. But God can speak to each human heart individually all the time—through His very presence. And this presence of His Love will transform each woman's heart in a special way. He has something specific designed for each one. And so I ask for the reader to take her heart and to present it to Him. Like this icon, I ask her to take her heart and lift it up to God and let Him place the Cross, His Light, His Life, and His image of Love within her as He desires.

Humanity is a creation wounded by sin, and only Jesus can heal these wounds. But in order for Jesus to heal and transform a human heart, a person must first present herself to Him, desiring for Him to do so. Each woman comes to this retreat bringing her life to Jesus as an empty cup. The cup of each life is different –some have chips, others cracks, others are too small, others are rusted and dusty.

And so by reading this book a woman is saying, *"I have this empty cup of my life and as I pray this retreat fill it, Lord, with whatever You want. Open me, transform me, fix me with Your Love so that I can be a source of Life to others."* This is not just an ordinary book that is interesting to read. It is meant to be prayed as a retreat. It is meant to guide the reader into a living encounter with God. The greatest word that is spoken here is unheard by the ears –it is hidden in each human heart that allows the Holy Spirit to enter and whisper His Love within.

Chapter 1

Stewards of God's Mystery

What does it means to be woman? Who God originally created woman to be is a mystery that many people have forgotten, especially in the modern world. St Paul writes in his first letter to the Corinthians, *"Thus should one regard us: as servants of Christ and stewards of the mysteries of God."*[1] In this retreat the Holy Spirit will give each woman's heart an understanding of the mystery of who God created her to be, and with this gift comes the responsibility of being a good servant and protector of it. She must care for it in two ways. First, and most importantly, she must live this gift that she receives. She must let God's wisdom transform her life. She must receive all that He wants to share with her, treasuring it in her heart, so that she can serve Christ as He desires, thus bringing Him glory. And secondly, she should teach others this mystery. This can be done in words, but most powerfully a woman can teach others through her example of life. If a woman knows through the Holy Spirit what God wants from her in life and she lives what He desires, then her life is like a book helping others to discover this wisdom and inspiring them to live the same. The mystery of woman is first explained in the book of Genesis when

---

[1] 1 Corinthians 4:1.

God created man and woman. In Genesis 1:26-27 it is written,

> *"Then God said: 'Let us make man in our image, after our likeness.*
> *Let them have dominion over the fish of the sea, the birds of the air,*
> *and the cattle, and over all the wild animals and all the creatures*
> *that crawl on the ground.' God created man in his image; in the*
> *divine image he created him; male and female he created them."*

This passage is key in understanding what it means to be a person. God created man and woman in His image. But He did not create only man or only woman. He created both man and woman together. God created man and woman differently, and their differences are important. God wanted for humanity to be in His image, but woman and man portray His image in complementary ways. Each shows a different part, a different face of God. If a woman reflects on her experiences in life, she will quickly see how many differences between man and woman that she encounters daily. Man and woman do not only differ in their body's physical structure, but they also differ in the way they think, feel, and interact with God.

The American Bishops in a pastoral letter *"One in Christ Jesus"* stated that man and woman possess one nature in two different ways. "Being male or female is a gift from God, not an obstacle to overcome."[2] John Paul II taught that "[i]t is only through the duality of the 'masculine' and the 'feminine' that the 'human' finds full

---

[2] National Conference of Catholic Bishops, Committee Report, *"One in Christ Jesus: Toward a Pastoral Response to the Concerns of Women of Church and Society"* (Washington, D.C.: United States Catholic Conference, Inc., 1993), p. 5.

realization."[3] It is very important that a woman knows what it means to be a woman and that she does not try to be like a man. This is because God wants to give the world the gift of His entire image imprinted in humanity, and half of that gift is given through woman while the other half is given through man. Humanity will only be a true reflection of God if women understand what kinds of gifts God gave to them and if they live faithful to these gifts.

This first Genesis story of creation shows that although the Father created men and women very differently, they both have an equal worth. Men are not more important than women, nor are women more important than men. They both have great dignity. And yet equality of dignity does not mean sameness. This truth should be treasured. It is a temptation in the world today for men to say, "Men are better than women," and therefore for women to say, "No, women are more important because …" So often in today's modern society the role of women is demeaned and belittled. Women are told by the media and the world around them that in order to be anything, they have to be like men. However, this is a grave mistake. The world needs femininity and the personhood of woman. Women have a special and extremely important role to play in humanity. St. Edith Stein once said, "The nation does not simply need what we have…it needs what we are."[4] And so, although both men and women have very important and beautiful gifts, these gifts are very different and must be respected and properly nurtured.

---

[3] Pope John Paul II, *The Genius of Women* (Washington, D.C.: United States Catholic Conference, Inc., 1997), p. 52.

[4] Herbstrith, Waltraud, *Edith Stein, A Biography,* (San Francisco: Ignatius Press, 1971), p. 97.

Genesis contains two creation stories, and it is only in reading both that one can fully understand who God created woman to be. The first story showed how God created woman in His image with a great, inherent dignity. And yet she was created with gifts differing greatly from those given to man. It is in the second story where woman can learn exactly which gifts God entrusted to her:

> *The Lord God said, 'It is not good for the man to be alone. I will make a suitable partner for him.' So the Lord God formed out of the ground various wild animals and various birds of the air, and he brought them to the man to see what he would call them; whatever the man called each of them would be its name. The man gave names to all the cattle, all the birds of the air, and all the wild animals; but none proved to be the suitable partner for the man. So the Lord God cast a deep sleep on the man, and while he was asleep, he took out one of his ribs and closed up its place with flesh. The Lord God then built up into a woman the rib that he had taken from the man. When he brought her to the man, the man said: 'This one, at last, is bone of my bones and flesh of my flesh; This one shall be called 'woman,' for out of 'her man' this one has been taken.'* (Genesis 2:18-23)

God said, *"It is not good for man to be alone."* [5] And so He wanted to create some companion for man. God created many different forms of life, varying plants and animals. But these were nothing for man, for even in their presence he remained alone and lonely. So, God decided to create a 'suitable partner'. He did not create another man. Instead

---

[5] Genesis 2:18.

God gave that man a sleep, and as he slept God took a part of his body and created woman from him and for him. There are two very important things to see here: First, that God created woman from man and from his need for someone to help him in his loneliness. And second, that God created woman for man as a gift. It is here that one can see the identity of who God created woman to be: God's gift and man's helpmate. The dignity of woman is shown in this passage because it speaks of how man needed someone and God created woman to be a gift—woman is God's gift of Love to man. A woman must remember two questions throughout all of her life, in every moment she lives. She should continually reflect asking, *"How can I be a gift? How can I be a helpmate?"* For only in being what God created her to be will she find peace, joy and union with Him.

God created each person with a specific purpose. But why should a woman strive to be as God created her to be? The answer is very simple. If people do not live as God wants, then their hearts will not have peace, and then the world will not have peace. Creation falls apart when it leaves God's plan. This truth can be seen in the example of a fork. A fork is a very important instrument. One could do many interesting things with a fork. He could comb his hair. He could work in a garden with it. But if a person uses it in such a way, it will not work very well because a fork was not created for those purposes. If a fork is used in a garden, it will be bent and chipped by the rocks in the dirt. If a fork is used to comb hair, one's hair will be torn and ratty. A fork was created to be used for eating. And so if a person uses a fork for eating, everything is in order and works nicely.

In the same way, God created everything in the universe with its own purpose and 'work,' even humans. A woman is free, and so she can try to be like a man or something that God does not want her to be, but in that both she and humanity as a whole will have problems. Humanity needs woman and all the gifts God has entrusted to her. And so it is very important that women understand and live how God wants them to live, so that both their hearts as well as the world in general has peace. For only when God's creation follows His plan can there be peace.

"The hour is coming, in fact has come, when the vocation of women is being acknowledged in its fullness, the hour in which women acquire in the world an influence, an effect and a power never hitherto achieved. That is why, at his moment when the human race is undergoing so deep a transformation, women imbued with a spirit of the Gospel can do so much to aid humanity in not falling." [6]

To think about:

1. In what way do I see myself created in the image and likeness of God?

2. Do I see the great dignity with which God created me?

3. What differences do I see in how men and women were created?

---

[6] This is from the first paragraph of Pope John Paul II's Apostolic Letter *Mulieris Dignitatem* where he quotes the Church's Magisterium that declared this in its closing message of the Second Vatican Council. The Council's Message to Women (December 8, 1965); AAS 58 (1966), 13-14.

4. In what ways do I see Jesus, Mary and Joseph living out those differences in their lives?

5. What false ideas exist in today's culture as to how men and women were created?

6. How can I live in order to help heal those wounds?

7. How can I teach children about the great dignity, giftedness and differences between men and women?

Chapter 2

Woman as Gift

Let us begin by looking at how woman is a gift. The person of a woman has many different entities to her: body, mind, emotion, heart, soul, and spirit. Women do not only differ from men physically. A woman's femininity stretches out and colors all aspects of her being. A woman not only is different from a man in her body, but she also has a woman's mind, a woman's emotions, a woman's spirit, and a woman's heart—womanhood is part of her entire being. St. Edith Stein shows one example of this when she said:

> …I would also like to believe that even the relationship of soul and body is not completely similar in man and woman; with woman, the soul's union with the body is naturally more intimately emphasized…woman's soul is present and lives more intensely in all parts of the body and it is inwardly affected by that which happens to the body; whereas, with men, the body has more pronouncedly the character of an instrument which serves them in their work and which is accompanied by a certain detachment.[1]

---

[1] St. Edith Stein, *Woman*, Vol. 2, Second Ed., Revised, Eds. Lucy Gelber and Romaeus Leuven, O.C.D., Trans. By Freda Mary Oben (Washington D.C.: ICS Publications, 1987), p. 95.

And it is precisely in the femininity of every part of a woman's being that she reflects God and is a gift to both man and humanity.

1ˢᵗ part of woman—her body:

The body of a woman is a gift. Can you believe this? How many women in the world today truly believe that their bodies are a gift? And yet this is true. It is very obvious and visible in the body of a woman how differently God created her from man. What is the difference between the bodies of man and woman? Physically, they have different sexual parts on their bodies. Man also has greater physical strength in his body to help him work (which is inherent to his identity as man). That is because God created man to protect, to care about his gift of woman, to do everything for his gift, to serve his gift, to work for his gift. And woman was created more delicate and weak, although strong in different ways which enables her to carry and bear life. The weakness of a woman's body calls forth love from her husband. Her need of his help (to carry heavy things, for example) awakens his needs to love, to pour out his strength as a gift. It is obvious in the physical bodies of man and woman how God created them to complement one another. And so, the body is a symbol for the entirety of the persons of man and woman. This is most obviously seen when husband and wife come together in marital love. Their bodies work very well together like a dance. The complementary nature of their bodies and souls is what allows communion to take place. God also created woman with the gift of the possibility of motherhood. This is a unique gift to woman which enables her to love and serve both God and humanity in a profound and intimate way. This gift for motherhood is something that makes her body very visibly different than a man's.

All these differences between a man's and a woman's body are good and beautiful. And yet many women today in the world have a problem with their bodies. Often, they desire for them to be more like a man's. Women worry about their bodies. And if someone is not comfortable in her body, it is very difficult to live. She cannot run away from her body. Television, films, and books all have very loud opinions as to how a woman's body should look. They say, 'All women should look the same with very thin figures." And it is just not possible for women to live up to such fabricated expectations. What culture often imposes on women is an idea of beauty completely different from how God created them to be. For example, society says that the hourglass shape of a woman's body is unattractive –and that a 'beautiful woman' should have absolutely no fat on her body. Inevitably, it says every woman should look like a stick. And yet, God wrote the vocation to motherhood into the bodies of women; and in order to physically conceive, any doctor will say that a woman's body must have a certain amount of fat in order to sustain the little, extra person growing inside. And so when a woman looks at what society says about her body, instead of looking to God (her Creator) for His instruction manual, she fails to see her body as a gift.

We must remember that God created each woman in the womb of her mother. Psalm 139 says:

"Lord, You formed my inmost being; you knit me in my mother's womb. I praise you, so wonderfully you made me; wonderful are your works! My very self you knew; my bones were not hidden from you, when I was being made in secret, fashioned as in the depths of the earth." (Verses 13-15)

I want you to take a moment now and close your eyes, and I want you to try to picture yourself in the womb of your mother. I want you to see how God himself was present there; how God himself took that little tiny body of yours and formed it with His own hands. And how He took your body and He breathed His own breath of life and love within you. I want you to see His presence with you within the womb of your mother because only in that will you understand the gift that you are in your body. You were created with the purpose of being a gift. **"Lord, You formed my inmost being; you knit me in my mother's womb. I praise you, so wonderfully you made me; wonderful are your works!"** Pray these scriptures and ask Jesus to help you believe them because each of you were created wonderfully, beautifully as a gift—it is a simple concept but something that rarely people truly understand with their hearts.

God's hands fashioned woman. He designed her shape and color and size. And He breathed His life into her—and in that bestowed upon her the greatest blessing and confirmation of her beauty: for in His breath entering into her, He chose her to be a temple of His Spirit. No woman can doubt her belovedness and beauty if she remembers that God spoke it by putting His breath within her. This was His way of saying, *'This is good.'* In Genesis after God created woman it says, *"The man and his wife were naked and not ashamed..."* The body of a woman without sin is not something about which she should be embarrassed. How God created the body of woman in the beginning is very beautiful. When God created woman, she was a gift. She was a gift just as God created her. And Eve, the first woman, did not worry about her body. She did not do many exercises so that she would look a certain way. She simply received her body and blessed Him, thanked

Him. It says that she was not ashamed. She recognized that her body was a gift for God (as He began to dwell within her), a gift for her man (who was able to work and rest with and in her), and a gift for humanity (who were brought to life and nurtured through her body). Why did woman begin to have a problem with her body? It was sin. Sin did it. And only in Jesus' redemption can the understanding of the giftedness of the body be returned to woman. Before the light of Jesus, before the light of God, a body in itself does not have negative connotations. It is God's beautiful gift. This is important for each person to know: that every body of every man and every woman is a gift from God.

In today's world, women are usually very wounded in their bodies. But God wants to heal women from this wound in a special way. Only in Jesus can a woman be healed to accept her body as a gift. If one looks at creation—say there is a flower and all the petals fall out; or say there is a tree and all the leaves fall down—a human cannot go and stick that all back together. There is nothing a human can do to fix creation in that way. But God actually can heal broken creation because He is the Creator. The human heart was created by God, and it has been wounded by sin. And each human heart has been wounded over and over by what the culture says, by what parents say (or do not say), by what a person has done (when a woman wounds her body in sin). But God can come and He can heal a human heart because He is the Creator. And so during this time of retreat each woman must take her body in a special way and give it back to God so that He can heal it.

A lot of healing can take place if a woman can go back to Scripture and find the places where God speaks about a woman's body. Sacred Scripture is God's Word to humanity, and so God is speaking directly to the wounded human heart through this book. In Song of Songs, God specifically speaks about the beauty of the woman's body. Each woman is God's beloved. And so each woman can find Jesus speaking to her in those special verses of Scripture, especially in the Song of Songs. Here are a couple of examples:

"How beautiful are your feet in sandals, O prince's daughter! Your rounded thighs are like jewels, the handiwork of an artist. Your navel is a round bowl that should never lack for mixed wine. Your body is a heap of wheat encircled with lilies. Your breasts are like twin fawns, the young of a gazelle. Your neck is like a tower of ivory. Your eyes are like the pools in Heshbon by the gate of Bath-rabbim. Your nose is like the tower on Lebanon that looks toward Damascus. Your head rises like Carmel; your hair is like draperies of purple; a king is held captive in its tresses." (Song of Songs, 7:2-6)

"Ah, you are beautiful, My beloved, ah, you are beautiful! Your eyes are doves behind your veil. Your hair is like a flock of goats streaming down the mountains of Gilead. Your teeth are like a flock of ewes to be shorn, which come up from the washing, all of them big with twins, none of them thin and barren. Your lips are like a scarlet strand; your mouth is lovely. Your cheek is like a half-pomegranate behind your veil. Your neck is like David's tower girt with battlements; a thousand bucklers hang upon it, all the shields of valiant men. Your breasts are like twin fawns, the young of a gazelle that browse among the lilies. Until the day breathes cool and the shadows lengthen, I will go to the mountain of myrrh, to the hill of incense. You are all beautiful, My beloved, and there is no blemish

in you." (Song of Songs, 4:1-7)

Every woman needs to find herself within these words of Scripture. These words speak about how God, how Jesus, the perfect Man, sees woman. Jesus is speaking to each woman, *"...You are all beautiful, My beloved, and there is no blemish in you."*[2] A woman needs to read this last verse at least five times every day so that she can have a healthy understanding of her belovedness in body. *"You are beautiful... without blemish,"* Jesus says. The language of the Song of Songs may be a little strange, but if a woman asks the Holy Spirit to help her look through that He can help her to come to know her beauty in a deeper way. Each woman must ask Jesus to help her believe these words about herself. Scripture is the word of God and so it can be very healing. A word is a capsule that carries a spirit to a person. And so the Word of God carries His Holy Spirit to us. When a woman reads these words they can carry God's healing presence into her. And so it is important when a person has a particular wound that she reads the Scripture that can help heal her in that regard.

It is important that a woman understands the beauty of her body and the dignity of her body so that she can be freed to use it as a gift, as well as so that she will protect its giftedness from the sin in the world. God created the human body very beautifully and for a purpose. It is the temple of the Holy Spirit—His Home. Look how God loves the body! A woman needs to keep and treasure this. Later, we will speak about purity, problems with purity and how a woman needs to treasure her body and live with it with dignity. But first a woman must know that she has dignity. God gave woman her body in order

---

[2] Song of Songs 4:7.

to serve—as an instrument of His Love in action as well as an instrument to reflect His image in the world. It is in this truth of being an object and instrument of God's Love that a woman's body finds its dignity.

2nd part of woman—her mind and emotions:

The mind and emotions of man and woman differ greatly as well. A man thinks very concretely. He has a very clear order. He is solution-oriented. This is because he needs to protect. In a difficult situation, man needs to cut through emotions and think very clearly to make a decision about how to act. He needs to know, *"Okay, we have a problem, so this is what we will do."* He must be a leader. God entrusted woman into the hands of man, and that means that man needs to be concrete, to receive that gift, to serve that gift, to lead that gift. A woman, on the other hand, lives more from her emotions and heart. The strength of woman lies in the emotional life. For through a woman's emotions she perceives what is happening in her soul in relation to God. And her emotions not only help her to know herself, but to also be keenly aware of others. We know that a woman generally worries much more than a man about people. A man may worry at times about work or about money because that relates to his primary job in the family: to provide a home, food, and security for his wife and children. But woman worries more about people because she is intimately emotionally in tune and attached to them because of her gift of motherhood. A woman also cries much more often than a man. She feels emotions very deeply. But this is because this is her gift—to feel very deeply. Why? It is because God created woman to be a helpmate, a servant, and a mother. If a woman helps, if she serves, if she is a mama—that means that she needs to be very sensitive all the time to what others need. Always. She always needs to know what her child needs, how she can help him, how does she feel, why he is crying. She always needs to know everything about that child. And when she has a husband, she must always know what he needs from her and how she can help him. She needs to help, to serve. And a woman knows how to help and serve through very sensitive emotions and heart. So it is a gift. Not only does a woman's sensitive heart make her more prone to feel the suffering of those around her, she also is gifted with emotions which easily spread joy, peace, and comfort to all. Because of her great, gentle love, in great crises of life a woman gives the great consolation. Fulton Sheen wrote, "When he is remorseful, sad and disquieted, she brings comfort and assurance."[3] Pope Pius XII wrote:

> God has granted to the woman more than to the man, through a sense of elegance and gentleness, the gift of rendering charming and pleasant even the simplest things, precisely because she, made like to man as a help-mate to form with him a family, was created to radiate joy and sweetness about her husband's hearth.[4]

The sensitive emotions of a woman do not only serve those in her immediate family, but she is called to use this gift to transform the world. Edith Stein said, "Women's mature Christian life is a source of

---

[3] Sheen, Fulton J. *The World's First Love, Mary the Mother of God* (San Francisco: Ignatius Press, 1952), p. 147.

[4] Papal Teachings –LEO XII, BENEDICT XV, PIUS XI, PIUS XII, *The Woman in the Modern World* (Boston: Daughters of St. Paul, 1959), p. 82.

healing for the world."[5] In this way, a woman has the duty to be the helpmate of all of humanity, reconciling it to God. Society needs woman and the femininity that her nature entails. Pope John Paul II says that 'without the contribution of women, society is less alive, culture impoverished, and peace less stable.'[6]

A woman's delicate emotions demand great care by those to whom she is entrusted. Her sensitive heart makes her easily frightened and saddened, yet also allow for her to quickly be filled with peace and joy. In encountering a difficult situation, a man needs 'courage' to defend or help woman. A woman, on the other hand, does not need courage as a man does. Why? It is because man is her courage. A woman does not need courage, she needs trust. For a woman, courage is trust. This is why it is so important for a woman to have an environment of love in her life, so that she can easily trust the one to whom she has been entrusted. This was true even in the Blessed Mother's Own life. She always had the care of a man. When she was born, her father Joachim cared for her. When she was a girl and entrusted to the temple (as tradition believes), the High Priest Zachariah cared for her. When she was married, Joseph cared for her. When Joseph died, her Son Jesus cared for her. And right before Jesus died, He entrusted His Mother to the care of John. Mary could fully be a woman because she always had the care of a man. And this is one reason why it is very difficult in today's world when a woman does not have a husband, a father, no kind of man to help her—in difficult situations she feels very alone.

---

[5] Herbstrith, Waltraud, *Edith Stein, A Biography* (San Francisco: Ignatius Press, 1971), p. 97.

[6] Pope John Paul II, *The Genius of Women* (Washington, D.C.: United States Catholic Conference, Inc., 1997), p. 27.

She, of course, can turn to God in such difficulties, but it is hard for her without a visible companion because God created her to have someone to care for her. If a woman is a religious, it is Jesus Himself Who does all for her, but this is why every religious needs to develop a strong relationship with the Person of Jesus, Who is their Spouse. If a woman is a young girl, it is her father who has that courage and protection for her. If it is a wife, her husband. Woman needs man. That is why God entrusted woman to man. And by being a gift, a woman can teach man what it means to truly give all of oneself as gift—what it means to truly love.

The mind of a woman must be very pure because she lives how she thinks. If she thinks very impure thoughts or about herself, she will live impurely or selfishly. If she thinks, 'I want a man for myself because I want to feel good,' then she will start to live like that. She will begin to wear very impure clothing because 'she wants a man for herself.' That is not being a helpmate and not being a servant. And yet God created woman to serve. And so if she only thinks about herself, who will she serve? Herself. And in that she is not very woman. God created woman to serve and so her mind must be pure and focused on God always; it needs to rest in the heart of God and to listen to how God wants for her to serve.

As St. Paul writes very clearly in Philippians 4:8, a woman's mind should rest in "...*whatever is true, whatever is honorable, whatever is just, whatever is pure, whatever is lovely, whatever is gracious, if there is any excellence and if there is anything worthy of praise, think about these things...*" What is true, what is good, what is pure, what is holy, what is excellent—that is where a woman's mind should always be. If a woman thinks of such things, then she can live a very good life and in this she is both a true gift of God and helpmate to all. St. Clare of Assisi said, *"We become what we love and who we love shapes what we become. If we love things, we become a thing. If we love nothing, we become nothing."* And I would add, "If we love God, then He makes us become like Himself." And so a woman must fall in love with God in order to become in her own ideal.

A woman has a responsibility to not only use her mind in a good and holy way, but also to train the mind, character, and hearts of her children. Every society is made up of people, all of whom are the people they are because of how their mother raised and taught them. For this reason, the task assigned to women of shaping society through shaping their children is one of the greatest importance. One Holy Father stated:

> [The mother] is [the family's] sun by her spirit of generosity and sacrifice, by her constant readiness, vigilance, delicacy and tact in all that touches the happiness of her husband and her children; she radiates light and warmth... [happiness] grows from the wisdom of a mother's heart: a heart which wishes to give only joy, even if it receives disappointments; which for humiliations, returns dignity and respect.[7]

3rd part of woman—her spirit:

A woman also has a spirit. A spirit is how we live. Because man does not usually have as deep or sensitive emotions as woman, his spirit may seem to be rough at times. He can seem to be rough because

---

[7] Papal Teachings –Leo XII, Benedict XV, Pius XI, Pius XII, p. 83.

he needs to be very concrete and clear. Man preserves the law and is an image of God's justice, but God created women to not be like men. God wanted for woman to show His merciful face to the world—to show equity and a spirit of kindness, gentleness, and sympathy. A woman must be very calm (gentle, relaxed) humble, patient, and meek. In this, she can teach the justice of man the mercy of God.

I want to speak here for a moment on the idea of meekness. What does it mean to be meek? In today's world, meekness is often misunderstood to mean weakness—letting others beat you up and not responding to that. And yet when you look up the word 'meekness' in Webster's Dictionary, it defines this word differently, as meaning "not easily angered, patient, gentle, courteous, kind, merciful, and compassionate." In this way, meekness is primarily an interior state of heart. This is very different from weakness. A person must be very interiorly strong in order to remain patient and forgiving in the midst of trial. And so, for example, if a woman finds herself in an abusive relationship, I in no way am proposing that in the name of 'meekness' she should stay in a place where she is violently abused. Pope John Paul II spoke often of how women need to have a gift to be a gift.[8] A woman must protect the gift of herself in order to be a gift. But she can always try to control her interior state and not be easily angered, or she can strive to be forgiving and kind in her heart even if she must remove herself physically from a situation. Such an interior state of forgiveness will only help a woman. Unforgiveness only hurts the one not forgiving. It puts a person in a prison of her own wounds and makes her unfree to go on and live her life. And often such a state only agitates

---

[8] *The Catholic Woman, Volume 3 – Wetherfield Institute Proceedings* (San Francisco: Ignatius Press, 1990), p. 18.

relationships causing more division and harm. And so by embracing a meek heart, a woman will always be free to love and will be a bearer of peace to the world.

1 Peter 3:1-6 speaks of what kind of spirit a woman should have. Here St. Peter writes,

> *"Likewise, you wives should be subordinate to your husbands so that, even if some disobey the word, they may be won over without a word by their wives' conduct when they observe your reverent and chaste behavior. Your adornment should not be an external one: braiding the hair, wearing gold jewelry, or dressing in fine clothes, but rather the hidden character of the heart, expressed in the imperishable beauty of a gentle and calm disposition, which is precious in the sight of God."*

A beautiful spirit of a woman can **change** a man. It can teach him how to be calm. It can teach him how to be humble. So, a woman has to live with that kind of spirit—a very calm, very quiet spirit. Pope John Paul II stated once that he invited women "to become teachers of peace with their whole being and all their actions."[9] And in order for woman to cultivate peace, she first must nurture peace in herself. "Inner peace comes from knowing one is loved by God and from the desire to respond to His Love."[10] And so in order for a woman to truly live with the spirit God desires for her, she must draw near to Him and allow Him to open up her feminine spirit by the secure presence of His Love. St. Edith Stein once said, "Prayer and inner silence could enlarge

---

[9] Pope John Paul II, *The Genius of Women*, p. 11.

[10] Ibid., p. 13.

women's spirit. Women ought to become 'broad,' 'tranquil,' 'emptied of self,' and 'warm and transparent.' Only hearts that are emptied of self can be penetrated by grace, with its power to form women into the loving persons they are intended to be."[11]

There are many reasons as to why it is important for women to live with the kind of spirit St. Paul describes. One example is a mother. When a mother has a child (even a child who is still within her womb), that child knows everything. He knows how his mother feels. It is not good for that child if his mother speaks very loudly. If a mother is stressed, her child worries or has stress and does not grow as he needs to grow. During the time within his mother's womb a child's body and emotions begin to form. If his mother begins to be loud or obnoxious when he is still inside her it is very hard for him as a baby to be calm. If an adult is with someone who is like that, his body begins to naturally feel stress. And how much more sensitive is a little child growing within his mother's womb? If a little child needs to grow, it is very important that his mother has a very calm spirit, both while she is pregnant and after he is born. Whenever that child cries his mother always needs to calm that child with a very quiet voice. Have you ever heard of a child being calmed to sleep by a screaming mother? A child needs love. And he does not only receive love through touch, but also a voice can 'touch' a child. A voice full of love can calm him. So if a woman speaks calmly with love, then her child will be 'touched' with that calm spirit and love and will grow calmly and healthily. It will help a child not to cry if his mother speaks quietly. This is true not only of infants, but also of older children. If a mother has a little child who is two years old, often that child is sensitive and throws tantrums simply

---

[11] Herbstrith, p. 101.

because he or she is two. If a mother is not calm when this happens, if she is loud or stressed about this situation, it does not help anyone. The child will not calm down. But with a very quiet, calm voice a mother can teach this child how to calm down and be quiet and humble. And although God especially gave women this gift of a quiet, calm, gentle spirit for their children, they need to live this gift all the time and everywhere. To a woman, each person in the world is like her child. And in this way, a woman will truly become a teacher of peace with her whole being and all her actions,[12] thus in turn fulfilling their "unique role to humanize society."[13]

It is most important to know that God helps a woman to live with the spirit He desires through His Holy Spirit. He gives her the gift of His Own Spirit. And a woman needs to live with a spirit like the Holy Spirit. A woman especially has the gift of the Comforter's calm, peaceful presence. The calm, gentle, quietness of a woman's spirit is one way that women are a reflection of the Holy Spirit. A woman can teach a man how to live this spirit because this is a natural gift that God placed within her. St. Paul encourages all Christians to live this saying,

"I, then, a prisoner for the Lord, urge you to live in a manner worthy of the call you have received, with all humility and gentleness, with patience, bearing with one another through love, striving to preserve the unity of the spirit through the bond of peace; one body and one Spirit, as you were also called to the one hope of your call; one Lord, one faith, one baptism; one God and Father of all, who is over all and through all and in all." (Ephesians 4:1-6)

---

[12] Pope John Paul II, *The Genius of Women*, p. 11.

[13] Ibid., p. 40.

By a woman's embracing her natural gift in this way, she can help guide humanity to imitate God. This is the spirit of woman. Do people in the world live this sort of spirit or not? Usually, they do not. And this is a gift that God wants to give humanity through woman. A spirit is something seen within what a woman does, how she speaks, how she thinks. It is everywhere. But to live with a holy spirit, she needs the Holy Spirit. She needs a very deep relationship with the Holy Spirit. She needs to be like Mary was—full of the Holy Spirit. In the Visitation, when Mary went to Elizabeth, Mary was so full of the Holy Spirit that He jumped from her womb to John the Baptist within Elizabeth's womb, in that way 'baptizing him.' When this happened and Elizabeth said, "Blessed are you among woman," Mary replied, "My soul proclaims the greatness of the Lord and my *spirit rejoices* in God my Savior…" Her spirit rejoiced! A woman needs to give joy like Mary did. A woman needs to rejoice in God like Mary did. That is her work as woman. She needs to be so full of the Holy Spirit that He is able to jump from her heart to all those she meets. "My soul proclaims, my heart proclaims the greatness of the Lord and my spirit rejoices in God my savior…" That is woman's work. She must proclaim with her heart and soul the greatness of the Lord by rejoicing in Him in her spirit.

4th part of woman—her heart and soul:

The part of a woman we will speak about now is the heart, the soul of woman. This is the very deepest part of a person. The heart of a person is the place where the deepest parts of her emotions, thoughts, body, and spirit meet. It is a 'chapel' or inner room where a person meets with God. The Catechism states:

Where does prayer come from? Whether prayer is expressed in words or gestures, it is the whole man who prays. But in naming the source of prayer, Scripture speaks sometimes of the soul or the spirit, but most often of the heart (more than a thousand times). According to Scripture, it is the heart that prays. If our heart is far from God, the words of prayer are in vain. (2562)

The heart is the dwelling-place where I am, where I live; according to the Semitic or Biblical expression, the heart is the place 'to which I withdraw.' The heart is our hidden center, beyond the grasp of our reason and of others; only the Spirit of God can fathom the human heart and know it fully. The heart is the place of decision, deeper than our psychic drives. It is the place of truth, where we choose life or death. It is the place of encounter, because as image of God we live in relation: it is the place of covenant. (2563)

How does a woman's heart need to be? A very beautiful example of how a woman's heart needs to be is found in Luke 21:1-4:

"When he looked up he saw some wealthy people putting their offerings into the treasury and he noticed a poor widow putting in two small coins. He said, "I tell you truly, this poor widow put in more than all the rest; for those others have all made offerings from their surplus wealth, but she, from her poverty, has offered her whole livelihood." (Lk 21:1-4)

A woman needs to give **_ALL_**. Fulton Sheen once wrote, "Woman is capable of greater sacrifices than man, partly because her love is less intermittent, and also because she is unhappy without total and complete dedication. Woman is made for the sacred, she is heaven's instrument."[14] God did not create a woman's heart to only give part, but to give all to God and through God to others. Fulton Sheen writes of 'woman as fulfilling *mysterium caritatis:* the mystery of love. And love does not mean to have, to own, to possess. It means to be had, to be owned, to be possessed. It is the giving of self for another. A woman may love God mediately through creatures, or she may love God immediately…but to be happy she must bring the Divine to human."[15]

Woman is called to fight against the possessive selfishness that original sin tends towards through her generous sensitivity, tenderness, joy, and compassion, putting herself at the service of others in authentic love. Pope John Paul II speaks extensively in *Mulieris Dignitatem* about how such service of women to their families, the Church, and the whole of society must be carried out in freedom, reciprocity, and love. A gift is only a gift when given freely from self-sacrificing love. Because of this, the only way a woman can be a gift to the world is if she is enabled to freely accept the task God has requested of her to be such a gift. God created a woman's heart for Himself so that she can give all of her heart to Him, and through Him give all to others. The heart of a woman needs to rest inside of God. Only when she rests in Him, she is able to give all. When a woman's heart rests in God, God fills every part of her body, mind, emotions, spirit, and soul. Only when a woman is listening to God can she be a voice for God to speak in the world. A woman so resembles the heart

---

[14] Sheen, p. 85.

[15] Ibid., p. 84.

of God when she fulfills her vocation to serve. "No woman is happy unless she has someone for whom she can sacrifice self—not in servility, but in love. Life to a woman is otherness. She thinks less in terms of perpetuation of self and more in perpetuation of others—so much so devoted, she wills to sacrifice self for others."[16]

And so, the heart of a woman needs to be open—not closed, not afraid, not for herself. It needs to be open to God and listen, as a mother. A mother is always ready listening to hear if and when her child cries or what her husband needs, how she can better serve. And when a mother sleeps, she sleeps listening. If her new little baby sleeping in the cradle next to her bed starts to breathe differently than normal, she wakes up thinking, "What is with him? Is he okay? Will he die?" She is so sensitive to sound—so attentive. That is how we need to be with God. He gave us that gift. And God wants to use this gift we have of sensitive attentiveness in the heart to help all others. A woman must be quiet in her mouth and very open in her heart to the needs of others, very open in her heart to what God wants to teach, to what He wants to say through her. The heart of a woman needs to rest in God and TRUST in Him. This is so that what He says to her she can do. The heart of a woman needs to always RECEIVE and say, "*Yes, I want what You want, God. I want to serve as You created me to serve.*" Mary, Mother of Jesus, was like this. God sent an angel to her and asked, "Will you be the mother of My Son, the Savior?" And she said, "I am the handmaiden of the Lord, whatever you want God, Fiat, Yes!" That is how every woman needs to answer God.

Not only is woman created to love in a heroic way so that she fulfills her vocation, but also because through such love she calls others

---

[16] Ibid., p 180.

to imitate it. St Teresa of Avila once said, **"Love draws forth Love."** Yet when a woman lives authentic love, reciprocation is never a condition for her to give it. St. Bernard of Clairvaux once said something to the effect of,

> **"Love needs no cause beyond itself, nor does it demand fruits; it is its own purpose. I love because I love; I love that I may love...it is not pure, as it desires some return. Pure love has no self-interest. Pure love does not gain strength through expectation, nor is it weakened by distrust."**

Love leads to the fulfillment of a person, and so a woman should want the object of her love to be fulfilled by loving. And yet "Genuine love hopes for reciprocity without making it a demand."[17] A woman's tendency towards absolute devotion, sacrifice, and love often leads them to serve the weakest, lowliest, and poorest, demonstrating service in a spirit of selflessness bordering on martyrdom. Such death to self is heroic. Pope John Paul II said that emphasis should not only be placed on famous women who lived this—such as Mother Teresa—but just as importantly on those 'ordinary women who reveal the gift of their womanhood by placing themselves at the service of others in their everyday lives. For in giving themselves to others each day women fulfill their deepest vocation.'[18] This is not to be confused with relegating women to the margins of society and reducing them to slaves. Such an attitude Pope John Paul II believes would cause women

---

[17] *The Catholic Woman, Volume 3 – Wetherfield Institute Proceedings* (San Francisco: Ignatius Press, 1990), p. 18.

[18] Pope John Paul II, *The Genius of Woman*, p. 57.

to be prevented from fully being themselves and living out their vocations. If this were to happen, humanity would have a large void. Women are called to give of themselves; not to be bound and chained against their will to perform simple actions for others. The freedom of the gift of self in love is what makes them mirrors of God. And truly, when women serve as a handmaid of the Lord, they are images of His Divine Love in the world. In this way, all women regardless of their state in life should strive to image the Blessed Mother and her 'Fiat'. Only in this way do they bring the Divine to the human and fulfill their feminine vocation. St. Edith Stein said:

>...*Must all women become religious in order to fulfill their vocation as women?* Certainly not. But it certainly does mean that the fallen perverted feminine nature can be restored to its purity...only if it is completely surrendered to God. Whether she is a mother in the home, or occupies a place in the limelight of public life, or lives behind quiet cloister walls, she must be a ***handmaid of the Lord*** everywhere. So had the Mother of God been in all circumstances of her life, as the temple virgin enclosed in that hallowed precinct, by her quiet work in Bethlehem and Nazareth, as guide to the apostles and the Christian community after the death of her Son. Were each woman an image of the Mother of God, a *Spouse of Christ*, an apostle of the divine Heart, then would each fulfill her feminine vocation no matter what conditions she lived in and what worldly activity absorbed her life.[19]

Pope John Paul II understands women to their depths, and he

---

[19] Stein, pp. 53-54.

recognizes their valuable unique gifts. In his letter to women, he explains their special talents particularly their 'unique capacity to see the person as an individual, to understand his aspirations and needs with special insight, and [her ability] to face up to problems with deep involvement."[20] Because of her self-sacrificing and giving nature, woman is often empty enough of herself to be easily filled with the Holy Spirit. This leads to the gift she beholds of inherent prophesy—of being a connector of others to God and His absolute Love. When a woman is in a conversation with another, she should listen with one ear to what the person is saying and with her other ear (or 'heart's ear') to what God is saying. If she is attuned to God through the Holy Spirit, He will guide and tell her what she needs to say to the other—what they truly need to hear from her. And in this way this conversation can be a healing experience for the one to whom she is speaking in the deepest way possible. God guides the heart of a woman in a special way towards an abandonment to love. Pope John Paul II writes that **"Perhaps more than men, women acknowledge the person, because they see persons with their hearts. They see them independently of various ideological or political systems. They see others in their greatness and limitations; they try to go out to them and help them."[21]** This reveals the spiritual beauty God intended to rule humanity. **Women take persons and grasp them at the heart.** There is a dignity for all people's lives which is treasured by women in all their relations to others.

A woman must entrust herself to God. The simple prayer of Jesus

---

[20] Pope John Paul II, *Genius of Woman*, p. 29.

[21] Ibid., p. 57.

on the Cross—"Father, into Your Hands I commend My Spirit"[22]–is something she can pray quickly and which is fundamental for her transformation by God. She should pray, *"Father, into Your Hands I entrust my body, my mind, my emotions, my heart, my soul and my spirit—my entire life I entrust to You."* If a woman can give that to the Father, then He can make her in the entirety of her being into what He desired for her to be from the beginning. Amen.

■■

To think about:

1. What are my gifts of my body that God gave to me? How is my body a gift? What is my body to God? To myself? To others? What kind of relationship does my body have with God, with myself, with others?
2. Where *does* my mind rest? Where *should* my mind rest? What kind of thoughts should I keep in my mind?
3. How are my emotions/feelings a gift?
4. What kind of spirit should I have? What kind of spirit does God want me to have?
5. How can my heart live in union with God?

Come dear Jesus, please heal my body –heal my emotions, mind, spirit and heart –in all ways that they are wounded from the world or my own sin. Help me see the beauty of your creation in myself. Help me be thankful for the gift of my womanhood, so that I can give that gift

---

[22] Lk 23:45.

openly and freely to the world. Please, my Jesus, possess me with Your Love. Help me to know You and Your Love for me –for every part of my body, mind, emotions, heart and soul –so that this knowledge can free me to be even more open before You in trust. Please fill me more and more with Your Holy Spirit –with the powerful gift of your healing and transforming Love –so that such Love consuming me may flow out from me and touch the entire world. "Into your hands I entrust my body, mind, emotions, heart, soul and spirit." Amen.

Chapter 3

Woman as Helpmate

We talked about how woman is a gift from God and a gift for man. Now we will talk about how woman is a helpmate. It is very important that a woman understands this most important work of service—to serve God and others. Woman is a gift because woman serves. God created woman as a gift in her body, emotions, thoughts, spirit, and heart—but a woman is only a gift if she gives herself. Pope John Paul II writes that '[i]t is precisely by making herself 'gift', that woman comes to know herself better and is fulfilled in her femininity."[1] Women were created to surrender and give of themselves: first complete abandonment to God, then selfless gift to their husband, children, and all people. Fulton Sheen writes in *The World's First Love* that "here is the essence of womanhood—acceptance, resignation, submission."[2]

In order for a person to properly understand and accept this divine assignment to women from God, one must first understand the basis of what it means to be Christian. Jesus came to be last, lowest, and nothing. His holiness is shown in His great self-emptying love that

[1] Pope John Paul II, *The Genius of Women* (Washington, D.C.: United States Catholic Conference, Inc., 1997), p. 26.

[2] Sheen, Fulton J. *The World's First Love, Mary the Mother of God* (San Francisco: Ignatius Press, 1952), p. 83.

served. Jesus said, "*The Son of Man came not to be served, but to serve and to give his life as a ransom for many.*"[3] Jesus calls all Christians to empty themselves in service imitating His life of total sacrificial Love. Women have this virtue of selfless love written into their very beings because of their gift of motherhood. A mother must serve her children—in body, heart, mind, and soul. And therefore women find it easier than men to fulfill this great command of Jesus that we "*Love one another*"[4] through "*laying down our life*"[5] for all those we encounter.

"Our Lady is the perfect example of this, for when God asked of Her the greatest favor of being the Mother of His Son, She responded by calling Herself "the Handmaiden of the Lord," in essence "the one who serves." In this She was already imitating Her Son, Who was to come as the "Servant of the Lord." Pope John Paul II writes in his Apostolic Letter *Mulieris Dignitatem*:[6]

> "When Mary responds to the words of the heavenly messenger with her "fiat", she who is "full of grace" feels the need to express her personal relationship to the gift that has been revealed to her, saying: "Behold, I am the handmaid of the Lord" (Lk 1:38). ... In the expression "handmaid of the Lord", one senses Mary's complete awareness of being a creature of God... At all times Christ is aware of being "the servant of the Lord" according to the

---

[3] Matthew 20:28.

[4] John 15:12.

[5] John 15:13.

[6] Pope John Paul II's Apostolic Letter *Mulieris Dignitatem*, Section II, § 5.

prophecy of Isaiah (cf. Is 42:1; 49:3, 6; 52:13) which includes the essential content of his messianic mission, namely, his awareness of being the Redeemer of the world. From the first moment of her divine motherhood, of her union with the Son whom "the Father sent into the world, that the world might be saved through him" (cf. Jn 3:17), Mary takes her place within Christ's messianic service. It is precisely this service which constitutes the very foundation of that Kingdom in which "to serve ... means to reign". Christ, the "Servant of the Lord", will show all people the royal dignity of service, the dignity which is joined in the closest possible way to the vocation of every person.

Women, in fulfilling this great command of Jesus, are a constant reminder to men of what Jesus the Master has requested from them—that they, too, freely choose to make themselves 'slaves' and servants to all. For the night Jesus washed the Apostles feet He also commanded them, *"If I, therefore, the master and teacher, have washed your feet, you ought to wash one another's feet. I have given you a model to follow, so that as I have done for you, you should also do."*[7] To serve God and humanity in such a way, a person must be first open and docile in Love, willing to forget oneself to the heroic degree of placing others' needs before her own.

In doing this a woman imitates Christ Himself and is a great portal of grace to all of humanity. This is the greatest way she acts as man's 'helpmate,' for she helps him by being a model of Christian Love. **A woman's most sublime vocation is "making the total gift, accepting a divine assignment, being submissive for Heaven's holy purposes.**

---

[7] John 13:14-15.

Not to be the handmaid of God lowers a woman's dignity. Woman's unhappiest moments are when she is unable to give. Her most hellish moments are when she refuses to give."[8] If woman held every part of herself for herself—saying for example, "I have a husband but I don't want children. I want my body for myself. I will not give all of myself to my husband, to others…," then she is being very egoistic. In fact, such an attitude is the total opposite of who she was created to be (one who receives, nurtures, gives and protects life). Instead of being a gift and helpmate, she becomes a parasite (which only cares about feeding itself) and a burden.

Woman was not created for herself, but instead for God and for others. Especially in marriage a woman and her body is no longer her own. When she was married, she gave her body to her husband and to God for children. When she entered into the marital act she was promising to give herself totally to her husband and promising to remain open and receive his life into her so that she could nurture it, protect it, and then birth it to the world. **And yet her body is a gift only if she gives it. She is only a gift if she accepts her divine assignment to give herself freely in Love.**

Woman is a helpmate in her body, in her mind, in her feelings, in her spirit, in her heart, and in her soul. First, we will talk about how God created woman to serve through her body. Most obviously, God created woman to be mother. God created her body to serve another person. When a woman is pregnant, everything changes in her body. Her body is for that child. She cannot live as she wants—she has to be careful of what she eats; she cannot drink a lot of caffeine or alcohol; she cannot smoke—it is very bad for her child. Her body is serving.

---

[8] Sheen, pp. 83-84.

Even when she sleeps, her body is always serving. It is a physical sign of how her mind, her emotions, and her heart need to always be: to forget about herself to serve and give to others. In that is love.

A body is such a gift, for it is the instrument through which a person makes one's love visible. A woman can do this in a special way in the vocation of marriage, for she is constantly making her love visible through her care of her family—in cleaning and cooking, in teaching and calming. If a woman does not get married but is consecrated or becomes a religious sister, she gives her body to Jesus as her Husband and to the world through Him. She is able to do these same things—cleaning and cooking, teaching and calming—for all those in the world who have no gift of a mother, of a sister, of a woman willing to serve them in love. In sacrificing marriage and entering into a special spousal relationship with Jesus, a woman can serve more people. Her body is a gift, her mind is a gift, and her feelings are a gift to help others. A woman is only a gift if she serves. To serve does not make someone weak—such death to self imitates Christ and therefore makes one strong in Him.

As I said above, we will not understand that vocation of woman if we do not understand the vocation of Jesus. Women find their vocation in Jesus. Jesus opens the vocation of women because He is a real man. When a man is a real man, then a woman can be a real woman. But if a man does not do his work, then a woman is not free to do her work. If a husband is not willing to lead his family, this work falls upon his wife—and such a work is a burden to a woman. If a husband does not work to provide food, shelter, and clothing for his family, the woman has to do these things—and this takes her from her primary vocation of 'being' mother in the home. Yet, even if a woman finds herself in such a difficult situation, she still has hope. For Jesus is always a Real Man, and if a woman has a really deep relationship with Him He can help her when she is left to do the work of men, and His Love can free her to be a real woman.

Jesus also can teach a woman to serve. For woman's service is not an exclusive calling reserved for the feminine gender. All Christians are called to live heroic service and self-sacrificing love. It is only that women possess this gift in a special way—and in living it they can inspire and teach men how to live it as well. Jesus came to earth to serve, and He called all Christians—men and women alike—to imitate His Love in service. And so we need to know from Jesus that to serve is not bad. The world says that to serve is a bad thing, that to serve means that a person is weak, to serve means that a person is nothing, is a slave. Yet service, in imitation of Christ, actually makes a person the child of God—the person He created one to be.

Who is a slave, a servant in our world's mind? The last, the least, the lowest, and least important person. But Jesus came to earth like that slave, that servant so that He can teach humanity to also be slaves and servants. He told us to make ourselves last. And we need to know that it is very good and very Christian to be a servant. It is not bad. Often in America, especially in the universities, women want to be like men. They want power, and they say 'We will not serve!' 'We will not receive anything from men!' 'We will not let them decide or guide us!' 'They will not protect me, I don't need men!'

That problem is not only American, but also stretches throughout the entire world to Europe and Russia and beyond. But the question is "Why?" Why are women so opposed to service, to love? It is because of sin. Sin makes a person think about serving herself instead of sacrificing herself to serve others. It is not bad to serve. Jesus served. God, in fact, created Lucifer as the greatest angel. And what did he do to be thrown from heaven into hell? Did he lie or commit adultery or murder? No, all he said was 'non serviam,' which means, 'I will not serve.' Service is so important, for only through the gift of ourselves can we truly become who God created us to be and give Him the glory He deserves. As the Church so beautifully exclaims, "Man cannot fully find himself except through a sincere gift of self." (*Gaudium et Spes*, 24)

God gave women the gift of service to teach men how to be good Christians. Women are examples (when they live their vocations) to men about how our relationships with God should be. To serve is not weakness! It is not weakness. **If a woman serves, she needs to be very strong because she needs to forget about herself. Weak people cannot forget about themselves. This is important: what does it mean to serve? To serve or submit to others does not mean passive non-decisiveness; it means, instead, to actively forget about oneself.** The world will say that to serve is bad and that women do not need to be like that. But truly a woman's worth is in her service… because she has to always continually forget about herself. A woman needs to forget about herself. It is something that takes strength. It is important in order to teach men how to be with God. How a woman serves man teaches him how to serve God. In the same way that a woman listens to what man needs and serves him, man needs to listen to God and serve Him. This is how a woman helps men and humanity on the whole to come to know and commune with their Creator.

And so, how should a woman serve? How should she be a helpmate?

First, women need to have a gift to give a gift. Mary Rousseau spoke at a conference for women explaining that the giving of self presupposes having a self to give. "The Holy Father's call to women to accept the vocation of self-giving love is also a call for women's self-development. (But this must be properly ordered). This is not self-fulfillment for the sake of the self, but self-development for the sake of having something to give."[9] So, women have the responsibility to properly prepare and form themselves to be beautiful gifts from God to their husbands, family, and the entire world. And yet what can a woman give the world if she first does not **receive** from God? And so to be a helpmate she first needs a relationship with God.

The greatest way that a woman can become a gift is to return to her Father and ask Him to form her and guide her. He needs to fill her so that she has something to give. A woman must have a gift to give a gift. She has to take time to be with God so that she can serve. She needs to care for her body—not worry about her body (not trying to look at it or care for it as an obsession)—but she does need to be healthy so that she can give her body as a gift. A woman has to care for her mind, so she needs education of some sort; she needs something that she can give. A woman needs to receive emotionally from God (for example, love, calmness, and peace inside her emotions) so that she can give that to others. Women often are 'all over the place' with their emotions—up and down, back and forth. That is how a woman was created—with sensitive emotions which must be tempered. But by imitating Mary and turning to God, a woman can find stability inside her emotions. For example, when a woman starts to feel really happy or excited, she should not yell or scream, but instead should allow her

---

[9] *The Catholic Woman, Volume 3 – Wetherfield Institute Proceedings* (San Francisco: Ignatius Press, 1990), p. 18.

heart to rejoice with God—to allow that joy to do something very deep within her. When a woman is very afraid, she should not scream and cry—but she needs to be calm and trust God.

A woman also needs to receive the Holy Spirit so that she has a holy spirit to give others. She needs to receive Jesus' Heart to herself— especially in the Eucharist—so that she has a heart to give others. It is through Jesus' Heart that a woman finds her heart, her identity healed by His Love on the Cross. When she receives Jesus—His Heart—He creates order in her heart, in her relationship with God, so that she has a heart to give God. This is how the Blessed Mother was. Her heart always rested in His Heart and therefore She was able to pray *"I am the handmaiden of the Lord...."*[10] This is why She became such a powerful gift for the world. A woman needs first to receive from God in order to give.

Secondly, a woman **needs to listen** in order to be a helpmate. She needs to listen, but to Whom? To Whom does a woman need to listen? First, she has to listen to God. She has to always be open and listen to what God wants for her life, how He wants for her to serve others. When a woman is a girl, she needs to listen to her parents because a mother and father want what is best for their child. A parent can be better than a friend, for their life experiences and mature relationship with God help them to see things a girl might not see for herself. Sometimes, a parent knows the child better than that child knows herself. As a woman grows older she needs to listen to people who God gives to her to help her—people who are examples for her and people who have experience, but experience that God has formed in them. In a marriage a woman also needs to listen to her husband. When a

---

[10] Luke 1:38.

woman marries, God asks that the voice of the husband is His voice for the family. And so a woman needs to listen to that voice. That is why a young woman has to be very careful whom she chooses to marry because the man chosen needs to listen to God and she needs to listen to God through him. If a young lady goes into a monastery, she has obedience to her superior. If a woman has a spiritual director or priest who listens to her confession, she needs to listen to him. In this a woman is listening to God through these people. A woman must listen to the Church—all her shepherds in the Church and all the teachings of the Church because the Church is her Mother Who wants only to give her Life. A woman also needs to listen to God in her heart through prayer. It is only through daily communication with her Father in Heaven that she can come to know all He desires of her life. Simply being in His presence through prayer is a form of 'listening'—for when a woman is docile in His arms, He can speak to her and form her simply through His Love.

So in order to be a helpmate, a woman needs to receive a gift to give, and also needs to listen to God through the Church, her parents, her heart, and her husband or superior. Only in this way does a woman know how to give that gift that she has, that she *is*. For example, if a husband decides something in a family, this tells his wife how God desires for her to serve. One day the husband may say, "I think that Sunday our family needs to stay home and not go out to our friends' houses, but instead be together because it is a day for our family. And I would like to eat lunch together and then go to the park. I feel strongly that is what God wants for our family." His wife needs to say, "I agree!" And so this woman has the gift of her body from God—the gift of a body that can prepare food. But her husband told her *how* God wants for her to use that gift; he said, "Serve through your body –and you will do this by preparing lunch." This woman received the gift of her body from God and knew how to serve with this gift from God's voice speaking in her husband.

Another example is a religious sister. She has a gift of body, too. Her superior might say, "Go make lunch for the poor homeless people in the street." This religious has the gift of her body from God, and she knows how to use it from listening to God's voice in her superior. A young girl has the gift of her mind from God. Her mother might say, "You understand the teachings of the Church really well; you have really good grades in religion class. I teach CCD to preschoolers on Sunday morning—come with me. Serve with me with the gift of your mind that God gave to you." And that girl listens to and obeys her mother through the gift of her mind that God gave to her to teach others. God can also speak inside of the heart of a person. Maybe when a young woman is at home one day sitting with her brothers and sisters and watching TV while her mother is preparing lunch in the kitchen, she hears in her heart somewhere God say, "Go, help your mother." God gave her the gift of her body, and He guides her through her heart how to serve with this gift.

And so a woman is a helpmate, a servant. And she can be this if she receives, listens, and most importantly—**obeys**. A woman can listen to the voice of her mother, her spiritual director, or her superior in a religious community or even God Himself—but if she does not obey that voice that speaks to her, what good is that? What good is it to listen to God, to God speaking through others, if a person does not answer Him—if a woman does not obey? Not only is a woman called to receive from, listen to, and obey God, but this listening and obedience always needs to have the source of Love—it needs to come from a heart full of love. So, in the fabricated story above, that wife could answer her husband in two different ways about the upcoming Sunday. She could say, "Okay, I'll do that. I wanted to go shopping all day Sunday, but I guess I'll stay home and be with you. But the whole time I will talk about how difficult it is and how hot I am and how I don't want to go to the park because my legs hurt from standing and preparing lunch for all of you." OR she can do this through the Holy Spirit with Love as God wants. She can smile and be full of peace and love, joyful that she can imitate Christ in sacrificial love in order to make her family more unified and holy. Which way does God want for a woman to be a helpmate? Always *in Love.*

God created woman so that if she does not serve, she is no longer a woman. He created her to serve all the time. And He wants for her not only to serve, but to serve in holiness, to serve in Love. In order to do this, a woman needs a very deep relationship with God. She needs to receive first the gift of herself from God so that she can hear what God wants and how He wants for her to serve and then to actually serve with His grace and in thanksgiving. God gives a woman the grace she needs to serve. And when she serves—when she uses the gift of herself for the purpose for which she was created (to serve, to give of herself)—then this service is her thanksgiving to God. It gives Him great glory. But a woman needs a relationship with God first in order to do this. **To the degree a woman is holy is the degree that she is a woman.**[11] Because to live the fullness of what God gives to woman, she needs a relationship with Him. This is not a question.

---

[11] Sheen, Fulton J. *The World's First Love, Mary the Mother of God* (San Francisco: Ignatius Press, 1952), p. 83.

Woman is a helpmate through many different ways. Woman helps humanity know one side, one face of the image of God. She helps men and the world know how they need to have a relationship with God: how to listen, how to serve, and how to obey. She helps through her body—she gives life. She helps through her mind and emotions—she is sensitive. She helps through her spirit—she gives peace. She allows a place for the Holy Spirit. She is silent and she listens to God. She is a helpmate through her heart because she allows God to fill it with His Love—she allows her heart to be a resting place for His Love to exist in the world. And this is the most important gift that a woman has—it is the gift of love.

Women have the gift of Love. And this is their greatest way of being humanity's helpmate. Women have the gift of Love because God created them to serve, and to serve is to love. To obey is to love. How did Jesus love us? He obeyed His Father and gave His body on the Cross. Women must love, and so that means women must obey and give their bodies, their minds, their emotions, and their hearts on the Cross as a gift to God and for others. They need to forget about themselves. Women have the gift of love for their children and for all others. Pope Pius XI wrote in his encyclical *Casti Connubii,* "For if the man is the head, the woman is the heart, and as he occupies the chief place in ruling, so she may and ought to claim for herself the chief place in love."[12]

Women should have 'authority' in love because that is the gift God gave to them. God gave men the gift of leading and women the gift of loving. Men have the gift of leading, of protecting, of guiding… but women have the gift of looking at others in love, from the heart. A

---

[12] Papal Teachings –LEO XII, BENEDICT XV, PIUS XI, PIUS XII, p. 36.

woman's sensitive feelings help others to grow around her because through them she is aware of the needs of others, how they feel, how they need to be loved. She knows how to love. For example: if there is a decision about one's children, a husband and wife need to talk a lot about this problem. It does not mean that a husband should not listen to his wife, he should. He needs to listen attentively to her, and then he needs to decide with and in the light of God what is the best decision for her and their family, what will give her and the family holiness. For example, he decides, "Our child cannot go to that party. It is not good for him. He won't be holy there." He can decide that. But his wife has the role to tell that child—to decide the best way to tell him in love. Why? The decision of 'what' is the husband's, the decision of 'how' is hers—because she is in charge of questions of love. She knows how to tell that child with love, better than her husband knows. And we know that. Many times men are very concrete, without feelings. They are solution and decision oriented and so may say bluntly, "You can't go. Period." But women are more sensitive. They say things in deep love and gentleness. A mother might say, "We don't want for you to be tempted, but we will do something else fun." Women are very peaceful in this. Women have this gift of love. And men need to listen and learn from women how to love in this way.

Eph 5:21-33 in a special way explains how women are to teach their husbands how to imitate God in Love. This passage of Scripture is the instructions of how a husband and wife need to be. This is exactly an example of how a woman needs to live receiving her gift, listening to how she should use it, and then obeying in offering herself in such a way.

"Be subordinate to one another out of reverence for Christ. Wives should be subordinate to their husbands as to the Lord. For the husband is head of his wife just as Christ is head of the church, he himself the savior of the body. As the church is subordinate to Christ, so wives should be subordinate to their husbands in everything. Husbands, love your wives, even as Christ loved the church and handed himself over for her to sanctify her, cleansing her by the bath of water with the word, that he might present to himself the church in splendor, without spot or wrinkle or any such thing, that she might be holy and without blemish. So (also) husbands should love their wives as their own bodies. He who loves his wife loves himself. For no one hates his own flesh but rather nourishes and cherishes it, even as Christ does the church, because we are members of his body. 'For this reason a man shall leave (his) father and (his) mother and be joined to his wife, and the two shall become one flesh.' This is a great mystery, but I speak in reference to Christ and the church. In any case, each one of you should love his wife as himself, and the wife should respect her husband."

Here it says very clearly how a woman needs to serve and obey her husband. But what it is really asking in that is that she serves and teaches her husband how to Love—both by being a living example of docile self-sacrificing Love and by calling forth her husband's Love by allowing him to serve her through leading. Here it also says, "Husbands, love your wives as your own bodies. You have to give yourself to make her holy." A condition of such obedience by a woman is her husband's sincere desire to serve her in return. And often a woman's willingness to receive her husband's service in such way actually teaches him how to pour himself out in such love—she inspires him by her courageous forgetfulness of self and awakens within his heart his need to pour himself out for her (his gift) in Love. A hermit priest friend of mine once spoke about this saying:

> Husbands must love their wives as Christ loved the church, laying down their lives for them in order to purify them. Men must crucify themselves for their wives. Women must expect from their husband as much love and service as Jesus showed the Church. The love of Jesus does not dominate us, but makes me myself, makes me free. In the same way, the love of my husband will not dominate me, but make me myself and free. So, in submission, a woman must be docile and accepting enough in order to receive the full service, love, and pouring out of self of her husband. Anything less is not worthy of her dignity. A man must die to himself in marriage. In love, a man must sacrifice himself to make his woman pure....

Men are called to love their wives as Christ loved the Church. This is a calling to husbands to give themselves fully as Jesus did. Jesus' whole life was for others. A husband's whole life needs to be for his wife. The only way a man can do this, can know what it means to love in such an intense way, is to live such a relationship with Jesus. This is why men must first live the mystery of contemplation, of deep union with God—so that they know how to love their wife as God loves them. A man must enter a spousal relationship with God. Otherwise, he will give only human love to his wife. But if a man can enter into the mystery of God, he can offer his wife Divine Love as well.[13]

And so, if a woman truly met someone who wanted to give his body, his heart, and his soul to make her holy, wouldn't she want to obey him? If he only wanted to pour himself out in service and to decide things in her life to make her holy, wouldn't she want to trust him enough to obey him? A woman's obedient, docile, trusting Love also needs to be lived in a religious life—the superior needs to listen to her sisters, those sisters for whom she cares; she needs to want to be the biggest Servant, the First Servant of all. She needs to search for holiness for her sisters. If a superior did this, it would be easy to obey her. When all is in the order that God desires, it is not difficult to listen and obey. It is not difficult if the one to whom a woman is listening and obeying is deciding things to make her holy. The problem is that life is not always perfect, and husbands and religious superiors do not always perfectly seek to make decisions to help their wives or sisters be holy. But through a woman's faithfulness in such trials, through her obedience to God and to what He wants for her life (if she listens to someone who God gave to her to listen to—even if they make a mistake and do not always seek what will make her holy, but instead what will make them happy), a woman can still teach them through her example. She can still help them grow in holiness by obeying when it is not easy—like Jesus did—on the Cross unto death. And so this is one example of how woman can receive, listen and obey, serve...

Woman's greatest example in the role of helpmate is Mary. The angel came to Mary and said, "Will you become the mother of Jesus,

---

[13] Fr. John Mary Foster, *Conference at the University of Notre Dame* (Notre Dame, Indiana: Fall, 1998).

the Savior?" And what did Mary say? *"I am the handmaiden of the Lord, be it done unto me according to your word."* She said, "Yes, I will receive the life God wants to entrust to me. I will listen. I will obey." This is an example for all women. Mary was a helpmate for all of humanity. And so, it is very important that women serve—that they receive from God, listen to Him and obey Him—in order to be bearers of the Divine to the world and masterpieces of feminine holiness like Mary.

At the end of this chapter, I simply want to add that **women should listen and serve through their doings, through action, but also simply through being who they are**. Women of course need to do things in life—especially womanly things such as prepare food, clean, care for their children, etc. But also in order to be the fullness of woman as God created them to be, women need to listen to God, to have a relationship with Him, to simply *be* with Him. And this 'being' with God must carry over to their relationships with people in the world. The greatest gift a woman can give her family—her husband and children, her religious family or those she meets in the world—is the gift of simply 'being' with them in love. A hermit priest friend explained this well saying:

There are two dimensions to the human person: work and love. Our lives revolve around work—manipulating an object to get a product. This activity can become an idol, which dehumanizes and hides the deepest part of man, being love. Any work one does God can do better at the snap of finger. But God cannot love for us; love is an act of one's own freewill. Love is the dimension of the human person that is most essential to being human. Oftentimes, people treat others like work, trying to manipulate the other to become what he wants the other to be. But true love is not transforming another; true love is to serve the other in what is most deeply his. It is to serve the mystery of the other. In love, I must respect the other; I am not free to transform. Such a deep personal love is the only activity capable of fulfilling a human person in all his depths. Only in God, love with God and through God, a person is fulfilled…many times parents talk about wanting their children to be successful in life. But what do they mean by success? Money, fame, pleasures? True success in life is when a person is capable of truly loving. The only measure of a successful parent is if he has taught his child to love.[14]

An obvious example of this from Scripture is Luke 10:38-42, the story of Martha and Mary.

"As they continued their journey he entered a village where a woman whose name was Martha welcomed him. She had a sister named Mary who sat beside the Lord at his feet listening to him speak. Martha, burdened with much serving, came to him and said, 'Lord, do you not care that my sister has left me by myself to do the serving? Tell her to help me.' The Lord said to her in reply, 'Martha, Martha, you are anxious and worried about many things. There is need of only one thing. Mary has chosen the better part and it will not be taken from her.'"

Martha worked and worked and worked for Jesus. She fulfilled her

---

[14] Foster, Fr. John Mary, Fall 1998.

womanly vocation of being a helpmate—she helped and served Jesus. She made lunch for Him and cleaned and 'did' lots of other things to serve Him. But Mary simply sat at the feet of Jesus and listened to Him. Martha said, "Tell her to help me!" But Jesus said, "Leave her to listen—she has chosen the better part." Here we see how Martha is a very good example of a helpmate. She did her work to serve. Martha was being a very good woman. But what happened then? Martha began to think about herself and she wanted help. She was being a helpmate, but she also was grasping at help. She did not think about others all the time, she thought about herself, saying "Why do I not have help? Tell her to help me!" She was trying to manipulate Mary in order to get the outcome she desired (which was help), instead of accepting the situation and her sister's decision to sit and listen to Jesus and just loving in that situation.

Martha's works were very good, her service was very good. Jesus did not say, "You are doing bad serving." Or "You should not prepare lunch." He blessed her work, for she was being a good woman in her service. But, when Martha started to look at herself, Jesus said, "No, No, No…" To be a woman first means to receive and listen and love. And **after that** to serve. Mary chose the blessed part, the better part—for she first sat at Jesus' feet to receive, listen, and love—to simply 'be' with Him. The deepest gift of woman is not in action, but to receive and listen to God, to simply be attuned to Him and love Him, to be open like that. And after that, yes, a woman is called to allow her relationship with Jesus to take root in service. But such service is the fruit of first sitting, listening, loving, and then responding to His desires.

What Jesus was addressing here was not the action Martha was doing, but instead reminding her where her heart should be. She should have been thinking about Him and not about her own needs. She should have been loving Him—imitating His Love—instead of accusing her sister. To be a holy woman does not always necessarily mean to 'do, do, do'. Sometimes God calls women to simply be with Him—to listen, to receive, and to serve through prayer and serve through prayerful love. A woman must commune with God to know how He desires for her to serve—and this relationship of a communion of love must be the center of her heart and the foundation of everything else. By first spending time with Him, a woman's service will be in imitation of His Heart and therefore will bear much fruit.

To think about:

1. Concretely in my life, how can I live as a servant and helpmate in life?
2. How can I listen better? And Who should I listen to?
3. Practically in what ways do I serve simply through being who God made me to be?
4. What are some feminine virtues of Our Blessed Mother that I wish to imitate in my daily life? (ASK JESUS FOR THESE!!!)

Glory be to the Father, the Son and the Holy Spirit...

Chapter 4

Woman as a Mother
The Gift of Receiving, Nurturing,
Giving and Protecting Life

Another gift that woman has is to receive, nurture, give, and protect life. This is a gift written into the very body of a woman. Only a woman can receive a physical life within herself from God. Wow. That is a really big gift. And this is a gift that is not only physical. It is a gift that a woman lives through her body; that is not a question. But she also receives life through her feelings, through her mind, and through her heart. A woman's mind 'receives life' through reading Scripture and allowing it to transform her thinking to be centered on God and others. When a woman receives the Eucharist, her heart is receiving the very life of Jesus, Whom Mary treasured in Her womb for nine months.

Women nurture life. Not only does a woman conceive children, but her entire body, mind, emotions, and heart go for nine months into nurturing that child within her womb. And once a child is born, a woman dedicates her whole being into nurturing that child into a healthy, holy adult.

Women protect life. A woman's body is created to treasure and protect the life growing within her. Her entire being is filled with an instinct that impels her towards protecting the life that has been entrusted to her.

And women give life. A woman receives life and then births that life forth as a gift for the world. She receives life from God and gives life to others. This is amazing! After a woman receives, nurtures, and protects life, she births life. She helps that life to continue; she continues to protect that life. A woman does not only give birth to a child one time (give 'life' to a child one time physically); from the time of the child's birth throughout his entire life, she needs to give him life continually. Maybe only once she gives that life physically in giving birth, but every day, every moment, she needs to give life to that child. She gives food from herself, she gives clothes, she gives knowledge, she gives love, she teaches, she cleans—her child can do nothing for himself. So every day she needs to give life to him. She needs to give spiritual life to him—that is most important. From the first moment inside of her when that child begins to grow—she needs to give all of herself to protect, to help that child grow.

When a person looks at a very new child who has just been born, she can see that this child is so delicate. Something as delicate as a tiny infant God asks woman to protect. God entrusts His greatest gift—that of new life—to woman. Fulton Sheen writes, "In the Annunciation, Mary is recapturing woman's vocation from the beginning, namely, to be to humanity the bearer of the Divine. Every mother is this when she gives birth to a child, for the soul of every child is infused by God. She bears what God alone can give."[1] A woman must receive this life with love and joy. If a woman receives life without these two things— without love and joy—that life entrusted to her could die.

---

[1] Sheen, Fulton J. *The World's First Love, Mary the Mother of God* (San Francisco: Ignatius Press, 1952), p. 82.

An experiment was once done in America with new babies. It was a very bad experiment. A group of researchers took two groups of children who had just been born. To one group they gave all that the children needed physically, but they did not allow for them to be held or cared for emotionally. The other group of children were given the same physical care as the first, but also had an additional thing—someone spent a few hours every day holding them. The first group of children almost died and had lots of medical problems simply because they had not been loved. Love is so important for a little child.

I remember hearing another similar story about the orphanages in England after World War II. There were many orphans left from the war, so numerous 'Homes for Children' were opened throughout the country. There was a great epidemic in that most of the infants in these orphanages died. The cause of this death was very simple. Although the caretakers at the home were physically caring for these children's needs, there were not enough people to simply hold them, talk to them, and give them physical love in that way—and so they began to die. This was true in all the orphanages in England—all the orphanages except one. What was different about this one orphanage? It was a cleaning lady. In this one particular orphanage there was a very sensitive, selfless, maternal cleaning lady. And after she worked her 8 hours every day, she would spend another 6 hours or so going from room to room and spending a few minutes holding each of the abandoned babies. She was not able to give all her attention to all of them, but she tried to at least give all of her attention to each one of them as she held them for a few minutes. And in the end not one of those babies died. It is very important to always give physical love to children.

It is always important to give spiritual life to children, too. A woman should pray for her children and pray for those children who do not have parents to care for their spiritual lives. This is because children cannot grow without this. The breath of God is the Holy Spirit—He *is* Life—so without the special graces of the Holy Spirit's presence (which comes through prayer), a child cannot grow and develop in life properly. As we already discussed, a child needs love to grow. And the Holy Spirit is not only *Life,* He is also *Love* Itself. If a child is raised in an atmosphere of prayer, he or she can become a very powerful tool for God to use in the world.

Women always need to be very open to life. At all times! When a woman is open to life, the entire world can be transformed. The whole world! There was a story I once heard about Mother Teresa. She was very upset by all the suffering she encountered in the world caused by AIDS. One day in prayer she especially cried out to God about this and asked Him why He had not sent a cure for this horrific disease. He answered her that He had indeed sent a person to find the cure—but this person had been aborted as a child. One person can have such a powerful effect in the world! And so a woman must always be open to life and rejoice in the gift when it is received. Each life contains a mystery of gifts not only for that little person himself or for his family, but equally to be shared with the entire world.

Do you know what one person can do if he learns to love? There was a saint once who saw Jesus and spoke to Him a lot. And one time Jesus said to this saint that if there were two or three more people in the world who loved as powerfully as this priest, then the devil would not have any power left in the world. Love is that strong! And where do people learn love? From their parents, from their mother. The very first teacher of love to a child is his mother, who holds that child in her womb in love. When a person is open to life, life grows throughout the entire world.

My earthly mother is a very good example of this. She was always very open to life. My mother had 13 children. The very best gift that my mother (and my father) gave to us was faith, but the second was all my brothers and sisters. This is because they are my very closest friends. We always have each other if we have a problem. We always can help each other. This is our joy. In today's world, they say, "Children are problems." In today's world, they say, "A woman's body is her own body. And if a woman does not want a baby it is not good to ask her to have one—she does not need one—she can have an abortion. This is her body and she can decide." No! This belief is not true. It is a lie. God gave a woman her body as a gift, but He took this gift back when she received life. Her body is no longer her own, it is God's to give as a home to a little baby.

It is not a joke to get married. When a woman decides to receive a husband, at that time she also says, "Yes, I want children." That is why God gave her a husband. If a woman discerns her vocation is to get married, it is for two reasons: one, it is to have a love union with her husband that reflects the love union of the Trinity. But the second reason, equally important, is so that their love gives fruit. It is important to be open to life. A man and woman get married to have children—to give their love through the fruit of love. In the marital act a woman gives herself away—body, heart, and soul—to God, through her husband. She says in her action of love—'My body is no longer my own. I give it to you, and I give it to God. May He give us the gift of life here." Her body, her action, her heart in the marital act says these words. Her body is the new home for a child of God. It is no longer her own.

The question of abortion is not only about her body—inside of her is a new person (with her own body) who needs to receive protection from her mother. It is very easy to do an abortion. If a woman finds herself in an uncomfortable situation and she thinks that no one will know if she has an abortion, why should she not just have it? If a girl has no money or is embarrassed or does not want anyone to know she is pregnant, she sometimes thinks that she can just have an abortion quietly. But abortion is a very big sin! This is a simple fact to some of us, but to many in the world it is a revelation to think such a thing. If a person does an abortion she is immediately excommunicated—she removes herself from communion with the Church. Why? Is not God merciful? Yes, God is very merciful and can forgive every sin, but abortion is such a huge sin (if she knows what she is doing) that a woman who does this hurts herself, closes herself, and cannot receive the grace of God even when God wants to give it to her. It is like that sin locks her heart closed. If she decided to not receive the gift of God's new life within her, which is the greatest gift, how can she receive other gifts from God. She cannot. She closes heaven from herself until she goes to Confession.

Life is such an important gift and responsibility. Married love is not only for the husband and wife, but also for the world. And their gift to the world of fruit from their married love is physical in children—the gift of children to the world. If a husband and wife do not have children, they are very sad. They can give love to each other, but for how long? They live for themselves where a child would pull them from themselves. A child teaches his or her parents deep sacrifice in love. In this way, not only is a mother or father a gift to a child—a gift that serves that child in love—but a child is a great gift to his parent, for he calls forth a limitless love which reflects the Divine.

I want to speak here now to women who desire to have children and are unable. Sometimes God desires for a marriage to have fruit through physical children, but other times He prevents a woman from conceiving because He has other children on earth who need a mama. He wants for this married couple to bear fruit through their love through adoption—either in a physical way or in a spiritual way. Sometimes, God will take a couple and bear fruit from their love by their life of serving foster children or children in a mission. Regardless of the form, a marriage must always bear fruit in Love in whatever way God desires.

God's plan for a marriage is best! I am not saying that a woman has to have 15 children in order to be open to life or be a good mother. God has a plan, and each couple must in their hearts be open to His plan. Every month a couple should pray and discern His will. There are times, obviously, for grave reasons that the Church allows the practice of Natural Family Planning—and only a couple's informed conscience praying united as a couple can discern how long they can use it and if their reasons are grave. Most important is for a couple to be open to God's will. Just because a couple is open does not mean that they will have a lot of children. I have heard of a woman who only could conceive 4 times in all the 20+ years of natural married life. I know another who thankfully was open to her 5 little children in the first five years of her marriage because after that she became sick with cancer and was unable to conceive more. My sister Theresa gives the best answer when people ask her (as a mother of 9) how many children she wants. She always says, "I want all of them. God has a particular number of souls in heaven that He wants to entrust to me, and I want all of them. No more and no less."

Motherhood is something God gave to woman physically. But it is something that even an unmarried woman (or girl) can also live—every woman has a vocation all of her life to be a mother. The gift of motherhood is something sewn within every woman's heart from the beginning. We see this in little girls, who already at one or two years old begin to care for a doll with a most mature, maternal nature. I remember even when I was in Africa where it is very difficult for little girls to receive dolls; the children pick up sticks and pretend that they are their 'babies.' There is something natural in a female that wants to nurture life as a mother.

A woman's gift of motherhood was given to her not only for her physical children, but also the entire world should receive a gift from her motherhood. An example of this can be seen in a woman's presence in the workplace. Although Edith Stein taught that "a woman must sacrifice her profession to her vocation,"[2] she did see an important role for women in the workplace when it was possible. She taught that "instead of simply functioning as a lawyer, doctor, teacher, or civil servant, a woman would always have the opportunity and the obligation to serve as a motherly companion."[3] Pope John Paul II hopes that woman's presence within the workplace and economy will transform it from brute and dull efficiency to a humanized entity. The Holy Father also encourages women to be involved with politics to the

---

[2] *"The Catholic Woman, Volume 3- Wethersfield Institute Proceedings"* (San Francisco: Ignatius Press, 1990), p. 99.

[3] Herbstrith, Waltraud, *Edith Stein, A Biography* (San Francisco: Ignatius Press, 1971), p. 180.

extent that it does not interfere with their vocation.[4] Edith Stein states that "if a woman's vocation is the protection of life and the preservation of the family, she cannot remain indifferent as to whether or not governments and nations assume forms which are favorable to the growth of the family and the well-being of the young."[5] In this way, one can see how important it is for women to be involved in Pro-life groups and work either directly or through prayer.

The gift of motherhood touches all parts of a woman's being. A woman has a physical possibility to have children. But God also gave her very sensitive feelings so that she knows what her children need. He also gave her knowledge—in her mind—so that she can think, 'How can I serve and love others as if they were my own children?' He also gave her a very sensitive heart that has the possibility to teach children how to love God. In a special way, woman has the gift to teach children how to love God. It is not only for her physical children, but throughout her entire life a woman needs to live this gift of motherhood. She needs to try to give life to every person she meets. She needs to try to 'raise' every person she encounters in a spiritual and emotional way. Every child she meets she needs to look at as if he was her own child. Of course, if a woman has her own children physically, that is her first responsibility—she cannot care for all the children in the world and neglect her own if God has entrusted physical children to her. This gift is serious and all of her life should revolve around giving life to and protecting her children.

My sister Karen is a good example of this. When she was first married, she and her husband Scott took in foster children for a few

---

[4] Pope John Paul II, *Genius of Woman*, p. 32.

[5] Herbstrith, p. 180.

years. Eventually, when she had her own children and they were becoming too old to keep protected from the foster children (who were wounded and therefore sometimes violent, sexually abusive, and mouthy), she had to stop caring for these foster children and focus on her own. Although she began to focus on her own children (her primary responsibility), she continued to love other's children in a new way—through food drives, adopting Christmas families, and prayer. And I would even say that the deepening of Karen's own motherhood (by focusing more intensely on her own particular children) eventually would serve the world's wounded children. She would learn things from her particular motherhood that could help her later serve others better.

Women, after they are mothers, start to be different to other children, too. They become mothers to all. The attitude of receiving, nurturing, protecting, and giving life is God's call to every woman, regardless of her vocation and place in life. Women can be mothers to the entire world. Women can give life to everyone in different ways. It is true, as we already discussed, that women have a right to insist on their dignity being respected, but women also have an absolute responsibility to work for the dignity of ALL persons.[6] Laura L Garicia said in a speech, "Since God has entrusted the human being to women in a very special way, women by nature seem to possess a deep sensitivity to the intrinsic value of every person."[7] In *Evangelium Vitae*, Pope John Paul II also writes beautifully on the call of women in today's society to 'Reconcile People with Life." He says:

---

[6] Pope John Paul II, *Genius of Woman*, p. 17.

[7] *"The Catholic Woman, Volume 3- Wethersfield Institute Proceedings,"* p. 128.

You are called to bear witness to the meaning of genuine love, of that gift of self and of that acceptance of others which...ought also to be at the heart of every other interpersonal relationship. The experience of motherhood makes you acutely aware of the other person and, at the same time, confers on you a particular task: 'motherhood involves a special communion with the mystery of life, as it develops in the woman's womb...this unique contact with the new human being developing within her gives rise to an attitude toward human beings, not only toward her own child, but every human being...'*(Mulieris Dignitatem)* [Women] teach others that human relations are authentic if they are open to accepting the other person.[8]

He goes on to speak about the inherent dignity of life that women recognize, and the love women have for people because of that dignity. Women do not look at usefulness, beauty, intelligence. Because of the graces God naturally grants to them to be motherly and accept children, they also accept all people with the same open love. Because a woman was created for closeness with her offspring, she has an innate ability to relate to all persons with whom she comes into intimate contact. She has an ability to foster new life in others that stems from her maternal nature. Mary Rousseau says that 'with that innate, sensitive, maternal insight into their individuality, we often know by a kind of instinct how to nurture their ability to love.'[9] Because women are gentler and by nature have a more refined

---

[8] Pope John Paul II, *Evangelium Vitae,* § 99.

[9] *"The Catholic Woman, Volume 3 - Wetherfield Institute Proceedings,"* pp. 23

sensitive and tender heart, they can soften society, torn by so many wounds. Pope John Paul II called women to heal such wounds in the world by their God-like, self-less love.

I would like to touch briefly on how a woman can give life to the world in specific ways.

How can a woman give life physically?

She can give food to others. She can give clothes to others. She can help others clean themselves or their home. A woman can do this to a very heroic degree in the ordinary circumstances of her life. It is wonderful to feed the hungry at a soup kitchen or homeless shelter, but it is also very beautiful to offer to cook a meal for a sick neighbor or elderly parent. It is beautiful to take the time to attentively wipe milk from the face of a messy youngster or to sweep the dirty stairs of another's house. Most importantly, a woman is called to use her body as an instrument to make her love visible to others—for the presence of Love always gives Life. When the human person has the experience of being loved a certain fire is lit in his heart, a lightness of spirit, a peaceful soul, a quiet energy seems to fill his whole person simply because he has been loved as God created him to be. In this way, each time a woman gives her love in an active way, she is 'giving life' physically to the world around her.

How can a woman give life mentally or emotionally?

She can teach others. Women naturally are wonderful teachers because they were created to be attuned to others—they were created to be 'teachers' of the world to the children entrusted to their care.

A woman can also give life through her words. Women have this as a natural gift. Many times a woman will see a picture that a child drew and her reaction is different than a man's. Often a man will say, "Oh, isn't that nice." But a woman wants to give life—so she says, "Wow! Tell me about this. How beautiful that green tree is. Why is that moon like that?" That is how a woman should be with children in order to teach them and to help call forth life from them—to help them grow. This is like when a baker makes bread—if he simply mixes everything together and leaves it, the bread will not grow. But if he adds yeast and kneads the bread, then it does grow. And so, a child only grows when his mother is continually adding the 'yeast' of love in her interactions with him or her. This is how a woman needs to be not only with her physical children, but also with all people. She must be this full of love to each little boy she meets, each homeless man on the street—even with drunk people. She needs to change the world through love like that. So she must be like a mother to all people.

Women have the temptation to speak too much, and especially to speak too much about people (otherwise known as gossip). Yet, if woman lives in accordance with God's plan, each word she speaks should give life. What does this mean? When a mother is with a child, a child does all his mother does. If a mother says something, her child repeats those words; he or she listens and does what she does. A mother has to be very careful about her words. Each word a mother speaks to her child forms that child into the adult he or she one day will become. But this does not only go for mothers. Every woman has this gift of transforming people through her words, if women would use this gift. Each word spoken must give life.

If a woman says something bad about someone, or she says something bad to someone, this makes them sad, and it 'kills' their character. If a woman knows something bad about another, and if she speaks of this, it hurts her (because of the sin of gossip), it hurts the one of whom she speaks, and it hurts the one to whom she speaks (for it gives rise to doubts in another's mind, it encourages judgments, and it does not promote the healing and peace a woman is called to cultivate in the world). Simply said, speaking such words does not give life to anyone. It actually takes another's life.

I remember a situation I once encountered in Siberia. I was relating to my spiritual father a conversation I had overheard that bothered me. One person was speaking to another about the failures of a priest they knew. I told my spiritual father that I did not understand why this conversation bothered me so much—what they were saying was 'true' (factual), but I did not think it was very kind. My wise father used this experience to teach me a lesson about truth. He said, "What they were saying, Mary, was not truth. Maybe it was factual, but it was not truth. Jesus is Truth. And so in order for a conversation to be true (something full of Jesus' presence and light), four things are needed. First, what is said must be factually true; second and third, what is said must be said to the appropriate person at the appropriate time; and, fourthly, what is said must always be said IN LOVE (not in a spirit of criticism). This is truth. This is like Jesus."

And so, a woman needs to give life through her words by following these guidelines. Every word must be in imitation of Christ. A woman needs to always speak with a great purity of love and goodness in her language. Each word must give life. Words are like capsules, which either contains the Holy Spirit (Who gives life and love through a person's words) or an empty (and sometimes even evil) spirit (which kills life and abuses love through a person's words). When one speaks to others, more important than the words that are said in themselves is the spirit within them that is gifted to others. If a woman's heart is resting in God and speaking with Him, in Him, then her words will give life. But if her heart is resting in sin, a woman's words will kill and take life. A woman must always pray and ask God to fill her words with His Holy Spirit. In this way, a woman is receiving life from God in words and offering this gift to others through repeating such holiness through her own words.

How can a woman give life spiritually?

When a woman prays for another, she is a mother to that person. Prayer gives life. Prayer is like 'shooting' the Holy Spirit at someone. And His presence always gives life. It always nurtures life. It always protects life and then has fruit by bearing new life. A woman can also teach or guide people spiritually. Having herself an innate ability to intimately relate with God, she can bring others to know and love Him in a similarly intimate way.

Two Types of Motherhood

There are two paths in life through which a woman can receive life from God and give that life to the world—and to protect it. The first is physically through being mothers, and the second is through spiritual motherhood. A girl can get married and after that be a physical mother. Or she give herself to Jesus as a spouse (in one form or another) and take all of Jesus' children in the world to be her own to nurture through her spiritual life and prayer. First let us speak about how a woman can be a good spiritual mother. A woman receives this gift of being a spiritual mother from God through prayer. Such a woman must be a woman of great prayer, allowing the great graces that flow down upon her from heaven to pour out upon the entire world. She does not hold all the grace of prayer for herself. When a spiritual mother prays, she is concerned much more about her 'children' in the world than she is about herself. She may pray for the strength she needs to be faithful in her vocation, but in general she should not pray too much for herself. She should pray for all the intentions Jesus places upon her heart. She should pray for the world, for the government, for those who suffer in Africa, for children who do not have anyone to pray for them, for prisoners, for people deeply lost in sin.

A spiritual mother's life of prayer always will give fruit in service. Sometimes, this takes the form of scrubbing floors in prayer within the quiet convent walls, where other times a sister may be called to go out and directly work among people in society. Yet always when a woman responds to a vocation besides marriage, she is still called strongly to a maternal vocation of a spiritual light in which she should nurture souls to God. This can be done in many ways. When women work in education fostering love of God into the hearts of their students, they fulfill their call to mothering. When women are consulted as spiritual advisors or for medical help, they also fulfill their call to mothering. Pope John Paul II confirms this saying that "in this work they exhibit a kind of affective, cultural, and spiritual motherhood which has inestimable value for the development of individuals and the future of society."[10] Because the most important aspect of a society is its ethical dimension, women hold a great responsibility in being the teacher and keeper of such a community.

Any mother—physical or spiritual—must always give love to her children. To be a mother is not something a woman does simply for a few hours every day. Motherhood changes the entirety of a woman's being. She *becomes* "mother". It changes her entire life. It is not something she can be 10 hours a day and then go to bed. If her child wakes up in the middle of the night and cries, she also has to be awake to care for him. If a woman receives a phone call from a spiritual child needing help at 2 am, she must care for (and pray for) that person. It is her responsibility. She is always a mother. Always a mother—that is very important.

A mother needs to be very calm because her child will be afraid and not free to grow if she is not calm, if she always has stress. It is a responsibility of a mother to give her child peace. It is important for a mother to always watch her child. This is true especially of little children (under 5-years-old, for example). All day when they are little they can find something dangerous, so a mother has to be aware and care for the life of her child. (This is true in spiritual motherhood as well—she always must watch and clear the path before her 'child' from spiritual dangers.)

A physical mother always needs to watch what a child has in his or her hands, what he or she is eating, if he or she is coughing, who is with him or her (are they dangerous people or safe?). A mother always needs to know physically what is around her child. Is the room safe or not? A spiritual mother also has the responsibility to watch what her

---

[10] Pope John Paul II, *The Genius of Woman*, p. 54.

spiritual child has in his hands, what sort of spiritual food he or she is eating, who is with him or her and influencing his or her life with God. A spiritual mother must always keep the 'room' of her child's heart safe from all dangerous traps. Motherhood (whether physical or spiritual) is not something for one moment. It is forever.

A mother needs to pray always for her child. If a mother prepares lunch, she must give that preparation as a prayer of love for her child. If her child wakes up in the middle of the night and she needs to walk the floors with that child, she has to give this time as a sacrifice of love for that child. All in her life needs to be a sacrifice of love, a prayer of love. When a mother takes her child to bathe him or her, she has to do this as a sacrifice of love. When she cleans his or her face she can pray, "Lord, clean his heart, too. Help him be holy. Help his heart always be as clean as I clean his face now." A woman can always find very beautiful prayers to pray as she serves her children.

Physical motherhood is the way that most women fulfill their God-given call to motherhood. This is a very important vocation, for physical mothers shape all of society and culture by the way they parent and form their children. The first two years of a child's life, the child desperately needs to be with his or her mother. (This is true in spiritual motherhood as well—when a person is a baby in the spiritual life he or she needs much more care and attention—closeness to those who are 'nurturing their spiritual life'—than people who are more advanced in the ways of God.) A child needs such closeness with his or her mother at this time because he or she needs her continual love, a sort of love that only his or her mother can give. A child needs that relationship with his or her mother. God did not make a baby as He did for nothing—in order to grow a baby needs a relationship with his or her mother. And that is why God made him or her 'attached' to her through his or her need of eating from her own breast.

God starts this relationship within the womb of the mother. But a child needs to know that his mother will always be there for him or her—there always will be someone to care for him or her. He or she cannot do anything for him- or herself, so he or she needs the stability of his or her mother's presence and love. It is very important for a child that his or her mother holds him or her often. The first year of a child's life—almost the first two years of the child's life—a mother cannot hold her child 'too much'. I know people think, "Oh, that will spoil the child, he or she will always want to be held." If a child receives such strong, constant love, if someone cares for him or her and holds him or her for the first two years (I, of course, do not mean that a mother can never lay her child down, but if a child cries she must attend to him)—then he or she will grow properly in his emotions and heart and for rest of his or her life will not need that kind of love. But if that baby just sits, if no one holds him or her, if he or she cries for a long time with no one caring for him or her, then that child will search for love throughout his or her entire life. That is often why boys and girls have sex before they are married. That is why they do immoral things— because often they did not have a father who cared for them, or their parents did not hold them or love them, and they need that touch. They need to know that someone is there for them and they are supposed to learn this as a child through physical love.

It is natural that a person wants physical love, but God wanted for each person to receive this through his or her parents when he or she is a baby. Such closeness between a child and parent is also the foundation for a child's understanding of God. If he or she received all the love God intended for him or her as a child through his or her parents, then he or she will naturally be able to love God powerfully and trust God deeper as an adult. A child learns about love relationships from his or her parents, and this later will flow over and help him or her to form a love relationship with God.

For this reason, a parent cannot hold a baby too much. Babies are very dear (when people first see a new baby they want to hold him or her). God made babies so small and beautiful so that people would want to hold them because that is what they need. It is important for a father—or someone who can give that kind of love and attention like a man—to give physical love, too. This is because a child needs both—motherly love and fatherly love. I know sometimes it is impossible for a child to have a father in his life (because of death or divorce), but then that child needs an uncle or other Godly male figure to love that child in a fatherly way.

I remember a very powerful example of this from my time serving in the missions in Siberia. One summer, we had a week-long Bible School. The littlest girl, Tatiana, who was about six or seven years old, was raised by a single mom. After the first two days a priest came to visit the children for the day. Tatiana clung to him, following him as a shadow. She had to always hold his hand and sit by him when we ate or gathered to sing. She adored his fatherly love—something she had never encountered before. That afternoon this priest had to leave for a few hours for some sick calls. Little Tatiana was heartbroken when she realized that he was gone. She threw herself on her bed and cried and cried for him. She refused to leave her room and would not eat. Her natural hunger for fatherly love had been awakened in her heart, so it was natural that she was upset when she could not receive that which her heart craved. She was truly desiring God, but to a little child, parents are his or her first encounter with Him. And so when she was cut from Father—a great tool of our Heavenly Father's grace and Love—her heart was broken.

It is so important that a child has the stability of a mother's constant love. Sometimes, there can be a situation when a mother needs to go somewhere without her child, for an hour or two, but she should not leave him or her for long. When there is a very little child, a mother needs to be with him or her always. And after the first two years the child still needs his or her mother, but maybe not as intensely—she can leave the child for a bit longer, but it is very important to allow a child to bond closely with his or her mother. We have many problems in America when women decide to work and place their children in daycare. I have worked in a place like that. And I have to say, although I love babies *a lot,* I could not give the kind of love to each baby that he or she needed—the kind of love their own mothers could have given. There were just too many children. I gave all myself, but I could not give what God wanted for them because I was not their mother. Depending on the day, there were ten children for one person or five children for one person. God gave such a special love to a mother so that she is able to give all to her children, all of the time. Daycare cannot do this. Others cannot imitate that intense love God places in a mother's heart. I really love my nephews and nieces. I can be with them a long time. But I cannot give them what my sisters give them—because God gave them the grace to be mothers, and He did not give that to me. He gave me the gift of being an aunt. He gave my mother the gift of being a grandmother. She is an excellent grandmother, but she is not her grandchildren's mother. And these children need both a grandma, an aunt, and a mother. One person cannot be all these things.

I do want to add here that it is totally understandable that there are situations in the world today where other people's sin (a husband or wife leaving the family, etc.) or a parent's sickness or death have put single parents in situations where they HAVE to use daycare. Or there might be a financial emergency in a family. And although such a situation is not ideal, it may be the 'only option.' I am not condemning such women in the least—for I know that God must suffer right along with your hearts in such difficult circumstances. In such situations, I greatly encourage women to only entrust their children to the most attentive and loving caregivers, and to continually entrust them to Our Lady. If a mother cannot be with her child, she should pray for him or her all day (offering her work as a prayer for him or her) and ask the Blessed Mother herself to help her find someone to care for her children. Such a mother should also ask the Blessed Mother Herself to look after her children while she is away.

Sometimes, a mother is tired, and she feels like she has no patience. In this situation, she needs to pray to receive the grace to endure. Because a mother cannot be a mother only half the time, she needs to always give. If her child cries all the time, she always needs to give. And God gives that gift of grace if the woman asks for it. **To be a mother means to die. Because to be a mother means to love. And to love is like how Jesus Loved. He died on Cross. He gave all His body, all of Himself to love. A woman finds her maternity there—on the Cross, also. This is because she also has to give all of her body as Jesus did as a sacrifice of Love. She has to become a sacrifice of Love in her whole life.** So often mothers suffer so greatly. And I believe Jesus allows this—actually GIFTS such suffering to them—so that their children will be holy. If a mother truly wants her children to be holy, she will suffer to gift such holiness to them. Jesus suffered on the Cross to gift us a possibility of holiness. And so in such an evil world with so much temptations and sin, a mother will oftentimes suffer greatly in order to have something to sacrifice as a prayer to keep her child close to God. I am not saying this to scare anyone—I am not necessarily speaking of someone's house burning down, etc... but true mothers seeking holiness for their children suffer in little ways every day. And if a woman understands why she is suffering like this, she will collect such difficult opportunities as beautiful flowers and treasures and offer them to God as a prayer so that her children can be with her in heaven eternally someday.

And so, a mother is a mother ALL of the time. A mother needs to change her entire life for her child. When a mother is pregnant, she needs to be very careful about her own body and where she is. To smoke and to drink a lot of alcohol when she is pregnant is very bad for a child—children cannot grow right in that atmosphere, their minds cannot develop properly. A mother needs to change her entire life for her child. To be around anger is very bad for a baby. To be around loud music or a loud TV all day is unhealthy for a child. But if a pregnant mother is calm, her baby will be calm. If she goes to Mass and receives Jesus' Heart in the Eucharist, that baby receives his first Communion, too. In that way she is like Mary going to Elizabeth. When Mary went to Elizabeth, John the Baptist danced in her womb from Jesus' presence. And so if a woman goes to Mass when she is pregnant she can give her baby Jesus' Heart! A meeting with eternal Love! If she prays the rosary when she is pregnant—she is teaching and giving the Holy Spirit to her unborn child.

A woman's body changes after birth. If a child is hungry, it is not important where she is, she has to feed him. Her body is no longer her body, it is her child's food, protection, home. If a child cries and cries, a mother has to give all of her love, emotions, and heart always. It is important to help mothers because to be a mother is very difficult work. A mother always needs to give all and be joyful about it. This is because a child needs joy, and his or her mother is his or her source of finding it. The world must really pray for mothers. It is not a joke to be a mother. It is a serious responsibility of Love.

The most important work for a mother is to give her children faith and love for God—to teach her children to love God. It is very important for a mother to teach her children always. Even when a baby is very little—three months old—a mother needs to take a book and show the child the pictures, talk to him or her and teach him or her to pray. People sometimes say, 'Children don't understand words when they are little, why should you talk to them?' First, children DO understand much more than we give them credit for. And secondly, children need loving touch, and a mother's voice is a form of such loving touch. So, if she is always talking and singing to her baby, it is like she is holding, caressing, and loving her baby. It is a form of giving love. If a mother prays out loud with her children, then she is sharing love with them.

A mother should always be teaching her child—not only things about the world (that is important) but also about God. A mother should whisper, "Jesus loves you. How He loves you." If a person hears something many times, they begin to believe it. For example, if I hear every day, "You are not beautiful. You are not beautiful," then I will begin to believe this. But if I read Song of Songs every day where Jesus tells me that I am beautiful and His beloved, then I will believe that I am beautiful and beloved to Jesus. And if I believe in my belovedness to Jesus, then I will live worthy of that belovedness. If I know I am a child of God, I will live like that. So a mother has to teach a child about his or her worth and beauty in love. When my brothers and sisters and I were little, my mother used to sing to us, "Mary is a good little girl, I love her very much." "Michael is a good little boy, I love him very much." And I think that this sort of love and affirmation of our goodness (even if we were too little at some time to really understand the words) helped us grow to indeed be 'good' people.

Children are not a problem. People for centuries have seen children as problems or burdens. We even see this in the Gospel when the disciples rebuked the parents for bringing the children to Jesus. They did not want to 'bother' Jesus with children. But Jesus replied, *"Let the children come to me, and do not prevent them; for the kingdom of heaven belongs to such as these."*[11] Children sometimes may cause problems because like all humans, they make mistakes. Children are still learning—that is their job. And mothers have to teach them with patience and love. A child needs love to grow. Sometimes, this love must be strong love—sometimes a parent has to give borders to a child, but always one's heart must love. If a child does something bad—if he or she hits his or her mother—she could be very angry at him or her. But what good does such anger do? If that child is two years old, he or she does not understand what he or she is doing is bad until his or her mother teaches him or her that. If a mother spanks her child from her own anger, that does not teach that child, and it is not good. A child learns and grows in love –sometimes strong love, but love. If a mother

---

[11] Matthew 19:13-15.

is very calm, patient and in her heart full of love, then she can take his or her hand and hit it saying, 'No, No.' But that little slap is done in love and therefore it helps the child grow. She is not doing this from her own anger. She is only disciplining from her own patient love.

Maybe a mother needs to use a strong voice, but her heart is calm and inside she almost laughs at the situation. If a mother yells because her own emotions are angry, this is not good—it is not love—it cannot teach a child. **It can scare a child into doing the 'right thing,' but it cannot free the child to choose the right thing freely in love.** Only love can do that. Children need to know that their parents will love them no matter what they do. Children need limits, and they need discipline—because they do not know such things unless their parents teach them. If they receive all they want as a child, they will think as adults that they are the center of the world. But in that discipline and obedience they need love. If a parent says, 'I won't love you…' that only gives fear. That is not good. Jesus won eternity for humanity through obedience. That was His Love for us—obedience. And so children must learn obedience through their parents.

Women are called to show all children in the world love, regardless of the cost. I remember when I was in high school, I worked a few nights a week at a child abuse prevention center. I watched between 10-20 children, four-years-old and under while their parents attended 'parenting classes.' The stories that came with these children would break anyone's heart. I remember the very first night I worked at the center. The first little baby brought in to me was about 9-months-old, yet very behind developmentally. His father had taken him to the doctor when he was 6-weeks-old for a check-up, and when he would not stop crying as infants often do, his father had punched him in the face and thrown him against the wall. The stories I encountered week after week were so sad, yet I was so happy to be able to at least bring a little love into these children's lives. I was surprised at how often people said to me, "How do you do that kind of work? Doesn't it depress you to work with such suffering? I could never care for children like that." And yet, such questions had never crossed my mind.

Of course, I never enjoyed seeing people suffer. But my mother had taught me at a young age (as we opened up our home to foster children—some of whom came from broken homes and unfortunately had to return to them) that giving a hurting child some love is much better than no love. The motherly love we show the people we encounter may be the only love they ever meet. Why would I deny them the chance to encounter the Face of God's Love simply because I was 'uncomfortable' seeing and serving their suffering? Plus, Jesus said, "*Whatsoever you do to the least of my little ones, you do unto me.*"[12] Maybe that would be one of the only chances I would encounter in my life where I truly could be Veronica or Simon bringing comfort to Jesus on His Cross' Path. Women should always look at each person as if he or she is Jesus Himself. The Bible is full of accounts of when people were good to others, they later found out that they were actually entertaining angels.

Love changes people. Even every day, ordinary encounters simply filled with Love. There is not enough real Love in the world, and people are aching for this gift, which God particularly entrusted to women. I am continually surprised as I travel throughout the world by how many grown people tell me that mine was the first authentic love they had ever encountered in life (in 50 or 60 years of being on earth!)—

---

[12] Matthew 25:40.

and that such love helped to change them. Of course, when a stain soaks for a long time in water, it comes out easily. And when people's wounded hearts are 'soaked' in love, they are easily healed. A woman must never give in to the temptation of saying that another's suffering is 'too bad' for her to care about and serve. A woman was created as mother so that she can share such limitless motherly love with all souls she meets. It may just be the only love they ever know. And each child a woman has—physically or spiritually—is given to her by God not for one day, but for all of her life. For the rest of her life, she has the responsibility of that child. For example, God gave me each person who encounters me at a retreat or reads this book as a spiritual child, and so until death I have the responsibility to love and care for them as my children entrusted to me by God. I need to care for them; I need to pray for them. If a person has a lot of spiritual children maybe that person cannot every day remember each by name, but she may say, "Bless, help all children you give me in life." This is true about spiritual children as well as physical children—a mother is a mother until death, and often beyond death. That is her work—it is not something that ends when her child is 18.

My family holds many beautiful examples of holy mothers. My sisters and sisters-in-law are amazing mothers. They teach their children constantly (not only facts, but also about love and life), they write the government lobbying for the protection of all life, their houses are very clean, their children well-dressed and well-fed, and they each have their own unique, but very beautiful schedule of family prayer. My mother had 13 children, but each time we met a young single mother, we took them to live with us. After my mother gave birth to her own 12 children (and lost her 13th in a miscarriage), she began to take in foster babies. When my youngest brother became entangled in a long court battle, she and my father loved him as their own 'little Jesus' for 2 ½ years before they welcomed him into our family through adoption.

My mother was truly a mother to the world. My mother was a 'real' mother. Even when I spent years serving as a missionary in Siberia, every few weeks she would send packages of food, cleaning supplies, medicines, and many gifts for those I served. She is a very beautiful mother—she gives all. Growing up, she would not sleep at night until all her children were asleep. And she always woke up before all. Why? It was because her work was to 'protect' and give life. If her children did not sleep, it meant that maybe they needed something, so she wanted to always be ready to serve them, to give to them, to protect their lives (she waited up for us when we were not home and prayed for us). This was her love. Most importantly she gave us to our Heavenly Mother. She entrusted us to her care. A mother needs to give her children to Mary because she cannot always be with her children, and she cannot be a perfect mother—but Mary is the perfect mother, and She can ALWAYS be with and protect a child. If a mother will entrust her children to Our Blessed Mother, then she can be certain that Mary will make sure that her children grow up to be 'she' or 'he' God created him or her to be.

God never wanted for a woman not to have children. God calls every woman to have children—it is just sometimes that calling is not fulfilled in a physical way. But every woman must be a mother. And that is why every woman needs Mary to teach her how to be a mother. A woman must ask Mary to pray for all of her children. Mary had been a perfect Mama—and so Jesus gave her to us. Maybe our mothers were very good, but they were not perfect. And we should not want to be mothers like our mothers. We should want to be like Mary. She is perfect. She must be our example. We must ask Her to teach us to be mothers. We need a very close relationship with Her.

There were many very difficult things that happened to Mary in Her maternity. When She was pregnant with Jesus She could have worried that people would stone Her because She was pregnant out of wedlock. But She was calm, She prayed and trusted. When Jesus was born, Herod wanted to kill Her son, and She needed to travel to Egypt in the night with Joseph. But She remained calm in peaceful trust. Mary even had to stand at the foot of the Cross and watch people crucify Her Son—with a peaceful, trusting heart She had to allow Her Son to fulfill His Father's will in death. She lived very stressful things, but She was still a perfect mother because She had a deep relationship with God. If we, like women, go to Her, She can teach us how to be mothers. And She can be an instrument of healing in our relationships with our children when we do not live and love as God expects us to.

· ·

To think about....

1. How can I be a mother? (How can I teach my daughters to be good mothers?)
2. How can I give life to people? (How can I teach others to give life to people?)
3. How can I protect life now? (How can I teach others to protect life?)

4. What does it mean to be a good mother? How can a woman be a good mother?

5. What is the greatest virtue in Mary's Motherhood that I would like to strive to emulate?

Chapter 5

Woman as Wife

Mary is the archetype of woman. She is the perfection of the woman-wife that God intended when He created Eve. Unlike Eve who disobeyed God, Our Lady trusted Him, surrendered to Him and obeyed Him fully through Her Fiat at the Annunciation. In this, She was 'woman' *par excellence*. She was the New Eve created to be the Gift, the Helpmate, and the Mother to Jesus, our New Adam. She was immaculately conceived and never sinned—and so She is exactly what God desired for 'woman' to be. Her identity reflects Genesis—and yet perfects it—and so She is properly referred to in Scripture as 'The Woman' in all of the perfect beauty that God intended when He created Her.

In the beginning, to be 'woman' was to be 'wife.'

*"The LORD God said: It is not good for the man to be alone. I will make a helper suited to him… So the LORD God cast a deep sleep on the man, and while he was asleep, he took out one of his ribs and closed up its place with flesh. The LORD God then built the rib that he had taken from the man into a **woman**. When he brought her to the man, the man said: "This one, at last, is bone of my bones and flesh of my flesh; This one shall be called '**woman**,' for out of man this one has been taken. That is why a man leaves his father and*

*mother and clings to his **wife**, and the two of them become one body. The man and his **wife** were both naked, yet they felt no shame."* (Genesis 2:18, 21-25)

It is of Mary –the Immaculate New Eve—that the Holy Spirit speaks of in Genesis 3:15, *"I will put enmity between you and the **woman**, and between your offspring and hers; They will strike at your head, while you strike at their heel,"* in Revelation where it is said, *"A great sign appeared in the sky, a **woman** clothed with the sun, with the moon under her feet, and on her head a crown of twelve stars,"* (Rev. 12:1) and when in heaven it is proclaimed, *'Behold the Bride, the **Wife** of the Lamb'* (Rev. 21:9).

In the Latin texts of Scripture—Genesis 2:23-24, Ephesians 5:25, 28, 31-32 (where it speaks of husbands and wives), and Revelation 21:9 and 19:7—the same noun 'uxor' (meaning 'wife') is used. This simply shows that the use of 'wife' in Revelation is not a mistake. To be a 'woman' means to be a 'wife'—a gift, a helpmate, and a mother—to God, to humanity, and sometimes to a particular man on earth. Perhaps this same word is used in the all of these places of Scripture precisely to draw our attention back to Genesis and what God's original plan was for woman—both in relation to man and then on (through living the 'sign') in her relation with God.

God used this primordial sacrament between the first man and woman, the first husband and wife, to speak to His people down through the ages—through the prophets of the Old Testament, as well as through Jesus', St. Paul's and St. John's voice in the New Testament. All throughout God used spousal imagery to woo His people into a love relationship with Him. In most cases in the Bible, the word 'bride' is used to describe God's spousal Love for His people—and yet in a few circumstances 'wife' (or 'woman') is used directly (Hosea is one example)—and this, I believe, is not an accident. In these places this word 'wife' is substituted purposely to bring out another 'color' and aspect of God's love relationship with man—something that holds a slightly different connotation than the word 'bride' or 'spouse'. It draws our attention back to the essence of who God created woman to be. Saint Pope John Paul II refers to this in his *Theology of the Body*, saying (Section 95:2): *"The love of God-Yahweh for Israel, the Chosen People, is expressed as the love of a human bridegroom for the woman* **chosen to be his wife** *through the conjugal covenant."* And later on in Section 95:4:

> *"The analogy with the love that unties spouses is strongly highlighted in this passage. Isaiah says: 'For your Creator is* **your Husband**, *Lord of hosts is his name; the Holy One of Israel is your Redeemer, the God of the whole earth He is called.' (Is 54:5) Thus, in this text, God himself in all his majesty as Creator and Lord of creation is explicitly called 'Husband' of the Chosen People.* **This 'Husband' speaks about his great 'affection,' which will not 'depart' from Israel, His wife**, *but will constitute a stable foundation of the 'covenant of peace' with him."*

The Pope goes on to say that God's Love is first a 'Fatherly Love'—but when that Love is manifested in the Redeemer (Jesus) it takes on a spousal nature with Him analogous to 'husband.'

When you look at the Hebrew and Greek texts of Scripture, a few very interesting correlations can be seen regarding the use of 'wife' to emphasize every woman's connection to Jesus—the original 'Man' from Genesis. The etymology of 'wife' means 'woman.' And in this primordial sacrament, 'woman'—as God created her to be before sin—simply is a faithful, pure wife to 'her man.' Maybe this needs to be discovered in today's society again. What does it mean in one's very source to be 'woman'? There is also something beautiful and deep in regards to every woman's vocation in regards to Christ—stemming from the Hebrew word for 'woman' in Genesis meaning that she was 'taken from her man' (as each woman wants to be born anew from the side of Christ), they 'cling to each other' (as each woman wants to cling to Him on the Cross), and the two become one flesh (as each woman can become one with Him in the Eucharist and in suffering love). It is 'woman'—the 'wife'—who was created from the side of man as a gift to him, to be a helpmate. And it is in the Cross that each woman is re-created from the Side of Jesus as a gift to Him, as a 'helpmate' in redemptive suffering. It says in Hebrew that *'the man and his wife were naked, but not ashamed'*—just as on the Cross Jesus calls us back to original purity—to be naked with Him in Love, but without the shame of sin.

Mary is the perfection of this. Jesus Himself emphasizes this by calling her 'Woman-Wife' in Scripture. In looking at the Greek Scriptural texts referring to both 'woman' and 'wife,' one learns that the Greek word for 'wife' and 'woman' used in Ephesians 5 about husbands and wives reflecting Christ and the Church is the same Greek word used by Jesus in Matthew 19:5, in Revelation 21:9, and 19:7, as well as when Jesus addresses His Mother in John 2:4 and John 19:26. There is an important mystery here about why Jesus chose that word ('gune')—to reflect back to Genesis. I think—in its original meaning in the beginning—the idea of being a 'woman' simply meant being a 'wife,' which simply meant being a spouse, a bride, a beloved of 'her man.' Mary was completely possessed by God and lived this to the full, yet all women are called to imitate her in this. Taken from the 'side of Christ' on the cross—and re-formed by God through sacramental grace into a 'second half' of Him, each woman needs to live as His 'wife'—as His 'woman' as spoken of in Genesis—one flesh and blood and heart and soul with Him—in the Eucharist, on the Cross—'clinging' to Him as spoken of in Genesis.

The word 'wife' takes one back *to the beginning*—simply to the reality of being 'who God created man and woman to be.' And it is Jesus Himself Who points us to look there for the source of our spousal relationship with Him—as He uses the same language. In fact, Jesus Himself in the Incarnation perfectly fulfills the prophetic history of Adam. Adam's relationship with Eve (in the beginning) points directly to Christ—the "Man" who fulfills what it means to be "Man" better than even Adam did. Jesus as the Husband of the Church starkly reflects Genesis 2:23-25—or better put, He *fulfills* it. For Jesus as the 'Word of God' left His Father in heaven and came down to cling to His 'Wife' humanity –the Church—to become 'one flesh' with Her (through the Incarnation, the Cross and the Eucharist)—this being the ultimate fulfillment of Genesis 2:23-25.

This is what is referred to in the Catechism (#1045) when it speaks of Christ's ultimate fulfillment of marriage to His Church, saying *'Those who are united with Christ will form the community of the redeemed, the 'holy city' of God, 'the Bride, the **wife of the Lamb**'''*. Each woman, in imitating Mary, should be an archetype of the Church – taken from the side of Christ—clinging to Him as His 'wife'—taken from His pierced side—and allowing Him to possess her—consume her—lay His very Life within her. *'The man and his wife were naked without shame'* (Gen. 2:25)…just as each woman is called to join Jesus naked on the cross—but who has no shame because there is no sin.

Women are called to fully reflect Genesis and this original vocation of man and woman in living out a marriage as 'wife' to her husband crucified. They are called to be 'little' by allowing Him to remake them in 'original innocence' simply by their union with Him. They are called to go back to the darkened Garden with Jesus—who entered it not to eat of the tree of life, but to be crucified on the tree of death (the Cross) to give us Life, to endure the darkness and bring light back to God's original plan, to 'work and toil' on the Cross (Gen. 3:17) as they painfully 'labor' with Him (Gen. 6:16) to bring forth life to the world. The origin of every woman's vocation is in Genesis—simply being 'she who God created her to be'—who He wanted her to be 'from the beginning'—who the Father re-created her to be from the side of Jesus on the Cross.

Each woman is called to conform to Christ and to be a reflection of Him, the true 'Man' from Genesis—as Mary was a reflection of Her Son and Savior. Each woman should be a reflection of Jesus' Mother – who He called 'Woman'—not to degrade Her, but to praise Her as 'Woman' as God conceived woman to be in the beginning. There is something beautiful to be discovered in the fact that at the wedding at Cana Jesus said to His Mother, '*Woman, what is this between you and Me?*' (Jn 2:4) –in Greek, this sentence meaning the same thing as '*Wife, what is this between you and Me?*' Could this Greek word—meaning both 'woman' and 'wife' instead of degrading Jesus' relationship with His Mother, actually be elevating it, transforming it? Perhaps it was at

Cana—at the beginning of Jesus' public ministry—that He stopped relating to Mary as 'His Mother' and instead started to relate to Her as 'Wife'—as she would eventually be the archetype of the Church, the "*Wife of the Lamb*" (Rev. 21:9).

It is beautiful that at the foot of the Cross, Jesus also calls His Mother 'Woman,' in Greek the same word for 'Wife'. Here, when their new spousal relationship is consummated by their hearts being made one through suffering, their union actually gives the fruit of new life— Jesus gives Mary a 'new son' (in St. John) to represent all of Her new children –who are the fruit of Her Love union with Him. And by a woman uniting with Mary, her Mother –under the Cross (and called 'woman')—she can become a tiny image of Her—the '***Woman** (the redeemed 'Wife') clothed with the sun'* (Rev. 12:1) in this dark world. We see this in an ancient homily in the Office of Readings for the Feast of St. Agatha, where Saint Methodius of Sicily writes that St. Agatha was the 'wife of Jesus' through her suffering and martyrdom with Him. He states: "*The woman who invites us to this banquet is **both a wife and virgin**. To use the analogy of Paul, she is the bride who has been betrothed to one husband, Christ. A true virgin, she wore the glow of pure conscience and the crimson of the Lamb's blood for her cosmetics.*"[1]

Each woman is called to unite her sufferings to Jesus in a similar way, and thus be made 'one flesh'—truly His 'woman,' His 'wife,' as well. This is what makes woman so powerful –it is in her littleness, her humility, her purity of being so fully conformed to Christ—that He is able to defeat evil through her. It is interesting that the same Hebrew word (*ashe*) is used for both 'woman' and 'wife' in Genesis 2:22-25, as well as in Genesis 3:15 where it was prophesized that a 'woman'—the

---

[1] Analecta Bollandiana 68, 76-78

'wife'—would crush the head of satan. And when reflecting on Rev. 12, it is the Greek word *'gune'*—like the Hebrew, a word identical for 'woman' and 'wife' that describes the battle with and ultimate defeat of satan. It was the woman/wife (*ashe/gune*) redeemed—perfected in Mary, Our Mother—who by uniting with Jesus, Her Son, in Divine Marital Love—a giving up of oneself totally to and for the other resulting in complete union—who was able to crush the head of satan.

It is in light of this all, that humanity should re-think the strength of the simple word 'wife' or 'woman' regarding the spousal nature of our relationship with Christ. It is in light of this, that each woman should long—like Mary—to live on earth as the little, humble maiden of Nazareth who stood courageously beneath the Cross of Her Son Co-Redeeming with Him. It is in light of this that Jesus has called every woman not only to be His 'spouse' or His 'bride'—but to live the absolute fullness of these words with Him and Mary of living on earth as the *'little wife of the Lamb that was slain'* (Rev. 21:9 and 5:8-9). For 'wife' adds a dimension to both of these words—it makes a 'spouse' feminine and a bride 'taken', 'possessed', 'known,' consummated. On the Cross, Jesus said, *'It is consummated,'* (Jn 19:30) and it is there where He recreates and unites fully to His 'Wife'—the Church. Mary stands with Him beneath His pain—one with His pain through the sorrow of Her Heart—as a witness fulfilling this truth. Ultimately, if Ephesians is our model of spousal love with Christ—and St. Paul chose the words 'wife and husband' to describe this—then there must be a rich meaning in radically living in a concrete way the fullness of what it means to be Christ's 'woman' and 'wife' as the Father desired for humanity in the beginning.

■■■

To think about:

1. Which verses of Scripture where the word 'woman' or 'wife' is used do I most closely relate to?

2. Why does being 'woman' mean being 'wife'?

3. How can a single or consecrated woman live out this aspect of being 'wife' with Jesus and with humanity?

4. How can a married woman best fulfill what God intended in creating a woman to be a wife?

5. In what concrete suffering in my life can I best unite with Jesus on the Cross? How can I grow in a spousal relationship with Him? How will this affect my relationships to others in the world?

Chapter 6

God's Call to Women

We already spoke about how women need to receive, protect, and give life and in that we talked very quickly about various vocations: to be a mother, a religious, a consecrated person, or a single person still seeking to find God's call for her life or waiting for His time to fulfill it. And yet, how does a person come to know her vocation? The way each woman discerns God's will for her life is as different as each person is from the next. Vocation is from the word, 'to call'. If I call someone (vocate someone), I ask something of them. A vocation is something God asks from a human heart—it is a gift He gives to a person. And so just as no two conversations are ever exactly alike, so, too, God's revelation of His plan of Love for a woman's life is never identical to the way He calls another.

When God created each woman in the world He created her for a purpose. And a woman's heart has to find this purpose in order to live in peace. It is like the fork example; a fork only works right if it is used for that for which it was made: to eat. In the same way, a woman will only have peace when she gives herself to the purpose for which God created her. It is true that God created each person free and that He does allow for a woman to freely choose her own path in life. And God will always bless her and give her the grace she needs to be holy, always, continually, regardless of which vocation she embraces. But in order to have a very deep peace in her heart, a woman cannot grasp at the vocation she wants.

It is true that a woman's desires are usually one path to knowing her vocation, for God placed such desires within her heart, but it is important that a woman never grasps at a vocation for herself. In the Garden of Eden, Eve grasped at the fruit which was forbidden to her for selfish motives. A person never should want to grasp at gifts from God. A vocation is a gift a woman receives from God. The vocation He chooses for her is what will make her holiest and happiest in life, but it is primarily embraced for Him. And so in order to discern one's vocation in life, a woman has to listen to God, listen to His vocation to her heart, listen to His explanation to her of why He created her, what He created her to do, who He created her to be, how He created her to love Him.

When God created each woman, He created her to do something in the world. He had planned for that one specific person to help other specific people. For example, if I live the vocation God has given to me, then there are specific people He has planned to give life to through my living out of my vocation. Through His vocation to me, I can help others become holy. If I live something other than what God has planned, maybe these people will never receive the love God had wanted me to give them in my vocation. We are all one body in Christ—we are all in union in Christ—and so what one person does is not only about himself, but it also has an effect on others. If I commit sin, you suffer. Even if this sin does not seem to be against you, you will suffer from it.

Each person in the world, in the Church, suffers from one person's sin, because we live in communion. We are one body in Christ. And so it is important that we live our vocations because if I live my vocation others will receive the grace to live their vocations. Because when I live my vocation, I live in union with God. And this gives a place for God to come and rest in the world. Woman's work is to give a place for life: look at her womb—it gives a place for life. Also she always needs to give a place for spiritual life to take root. **If a woman lives her vocation, she is in union with God, and the Holy Spirit has a place (in her heart) to live on the earth from which He can work.** The world receives peace in this. A woman who lives her vocation gives peace. She enlightens the whole world with peace.

And so how exactly does a woman discern which vocation God wants for her life?

First, if the word vocation is from the verb 'to call,' what does a woman need to do? She needs to listen to God's call. She does not know by herself what God wants from her, what He wants to give to her. But God will tell her, He will call her, if her heart is open. In the Gospel of Matthew 19:16-22, there is a story about a vocation to a young person. This is a good example for all people:

> *Now someone approached him and said, 'Teacher, what good must I do to gain eternal life?' He answered him, 'Why do you ask me about the good? There is only One who is good. If you wish to enter into life, keep the commandments.' He asked him, 'Which ones?' and Jesus replied, 'You shall not kill; you shall not commit adultery; you shall not steal; you shall not bear false witness; honor your father and your mother'; and 'You shall love your neighbor as yourself.' The young man said to him, 'All of these I have observed. What still do I lack?' Jesus said to him, 'If you wish to be perfect, go, sell what you have and give to the poor, and you will have treasure*

in heaven. Then come, follow me.' When the young man heard this statement, he went away sad, for he had many possessions."

And so what happened in this story? A young man went to Jesus and said, *'What do I need to do to gain eternal life? What do I need to do to be holy?'*

This is every woman's question as well. Each person wants to know what she needs to do to get to heaven.

Jesus answers, *"You need to keep the Commandments."*

Most people know the Ten Commandments. And many would respond to Jesus as the rich, young man saying, *"I follow these, I am not bad, I don't steal, I love God, I obey my parents, I obey God."*

But Jesus said to him, *"You want to be perfect?"* And he said, *"Yes, I want to be perfect."*

This is the key: a woman must want to be perfect. Jesus said, *"Be perfect as my heavenly Father is perfect."* And a woman must want to follow this command of Jesus. When a woman is perfect, her heart will be at peace. Does this mean that she will never sin? No, she will. All humans are weak and inevitably fall. But if a woman goes to Confession and tries to be perfect in love, then she will have peace in her heart. Jesus wants for each woman to be perfect. Each person can reach perfection through the combination of action and mercy. Where a person fails to meet perfection in action and thought, she can meet perfection in the mercy and forgiveness Jesus pours out upon an open heart desiring forgiveness. In allowing Jesus' mercy and forgiveness to pour out upon her contrite heart, a woman is allowing Jesus to make up what is lacking in her perfection.

Jesus wants each woman's love to be so strong that she wants to be one with Him. If two people love each other deeply, it is not enough for them to see each other once a week for lunch. They want to be one—together always, talk always, to have hearts that know each other very deeply. If a husband and wife love each other, it is not enough to ride in a car together—they want to speak, they want to be one in body, they want total union with each other. And this is a sign of how a woman needs to want to be with God—how she needs to desire perfect union with God. Only in this will she find peace because God created her to be in that kind of union with Him. A woman's heart will feel empty without that kind of union with God.

And so returning to the Gospel story above, at first Jesus says, "*Oh... you want to be perfect?*" And in this question He was saying to the man, "*Oh... you want to love me?*" Simply keeping the commandments is good—but a living relationship with God is not only about following rules. It is about Love. Commandments help a person know how one needs to love Him, but Jesus wanted to show that rich young man that his true desire was a desire to love Jesus. Jesus wanted that man to see that his own heart's real desire was one of love. In His question Jesus is saying, "*Look, child, your heart is searching to love.*"

And the young man says, "*Yes, I want; I want to be perfect, I want to love.*"

Jesus continued, '*If you wish to be perfect, go, sell what you have and give to the poor, and you will have treasure in heaven. Then come, follow me.*' Jesus did not ask for half of this man's life or heart, He asks for ALL. Jesus said, "*Give away ALL you have, and take me, follow me.*" This story in Mark's Gospel portrays this encounter in another light. In Mark 10:21 it is written, "*Jesus, looking at him, loved him and said to him, 'You are lacking in one thing. Go, sell what you have, and give to the poor and you will have treasure in heaven; then come, follow me.' At that statement his face fell, and he went away sad, for he had many possessions."* Jesus **looking at him, loved him** and said, "*You want to be perfect? Give away EVERYTHING and come follow me.*" And that young man looked at his things, at his own life and was sad. He looked at himself and said, '*This is too hard,*' and he left Jesus. He did not look at Jesus Who looked at Him in Love. Jesus looked at him **with Love**, but instead he looked at himself. And therefore he could not receive his vocation. He did not look at Jesus. If Jesus calls a woman to something, to a vocation, He always gives her the grace she needs to do that thing through His Love, through His look. But a woman has to look at Him and not at herself in order to receive His grace. Jesus said, "*For human beings it is impossible, but not for God. All things are possible for God.*" *(Mark 10:27)* All is possible with God.

What does this passage mean for a woman's life? Does God want that all women become religious sisters or that all give everything to the poor? No, because that is not every woman's specific vocation. But God wants for each woman to give all that is inside of her heart to Him, and then with Him to others. He wants for each woman to only hold onto Him and His will in her life. He wants for her to obey Him. That is what Jesus is trying to teach in this Gospel. Maybe not every woman will be called to be like St. Francis and go to live in the streets tomorrow and to give away all that she has in order to be naked like Francis was. That is not everyone's vocation. But God does want for a woman's heart to be free from clinging to things. A woman should not cling to one thing in this world, not one person except for Jesus Himself. Jesus does not even want for a woman to cling to good people.

God said, "*Love Me with ALL your strength, and mind and heart—with ALL.*" **He does not want half**. That young man gave God half—he followed the Commandments. But where was his heart? His love?

God gave humanity half of what it needs to get to heaven through the Old Testament. He gave humanity rules, and that was half of the help it needed. But God's Love that fulfilled that law was through the Cross of His Son, through His death and resurrection. God did not give humanity half. Jesus could have only given one drop of His blood, and the entire world would have been saved. But **Jesus did not give half, He gave ALL because He loved and He obeyed**. So, for a woman to know her vocation she has to first love God as a Person with all of her heart. She cannot just 'love God' in a generic way. She has a Father in heaven closer to her than any person she knows. She has a Brother Jesus. The Holy Spirit is a Person living among God's children on earth—He is sitting here with each woman as she reads this. At the beginning of this book, we prayed asking the Holy Spirit to come, and He came. Because He also obeys—He is love, and love obeys. Jesus said, "*If you ask for the Holy Spirit I will send Him.*" And we asked, so He sent Him. He is here as a Person with each woman as she reads. A woman needs to know God as a Person so that she can enter into a love relationship with Him.

And so, how will a woman discover her vocation? She must do the opposite of the rich young man. She must look at Jesus on the Cross Who loves her and Who gives her all the strength and grace she needs to do all that He asks. Jesus does not ask things from a person so that she will be sad. One might say, "He wants me to be His wife, but I don't want to be a religious sister because I want my own children." But does such a woman truly have any idea of what it means to be Jesus' wife?

He wants for each person to be happy. If God created his child to be a religious sister, she must go to Him! She will be full of peace and love and joy and happiness in this way. But if she does her own will, although He will bless her and try to help her also have a good life, her heart will always have something empty in it because God created her for something else. The same is true if God created a woman to be married—she will not fulfill her life's vocation in any other way. But regardless of what vocation God calls a woman to live, she must first go to Jesus, fall in Love with Him and give Him everything.

To be a holy wife of a man here on earth and to be a holy mother, she needs to enter that vocation because God asked her to do it. Not because she wanted a husband for herself or because she wanted children for herself. These are very good things: a husband and children are holy things that God created in Genesis. In paradise, God created man and woman to be together. But if a person takes these things because she wants them (disregarding what God wants), then that choice is egoistic—it is to live for herself, to do something only for herself. And God told humanity that it must live for Him. Every woman must live for Jesus. And she must be full of joy to be only for Him her whole life. And only after that if her first Love, Jesus, says to her, "Love Me in that husband that I will send to you," then it is very beautiful and good that she gets married. Because she does this in obedience to her Savior, her Father, her First Love. And she loves Jesus inside that husband because Jesus asked her to do this.

It is important for a woman to wait until Jesus tells her what He wants for her life and not to worry about an answer to the question of one's vocation quickly. It is such a temptation to fear and worry about finding a husband quickly—this is a panic in the United States, but even more so true in other countries. In Russia, for example, there are three women for every man. And so it is like a war for any young lady if she wants to find a husband for herself. And yet it must be explained to these girls (as it must be explained to any American lady as well), if a woman wants a husband because Jesus wants that for her, He will find him for her and He will send him to her. And this husband will be holy because Jesus chose him for her, and this husband will want to help make her holy.

A vocation is one's path to heaven. It is not to receive happiness on earth (even if one's vocation gives her joy). The purpose of a woman's vocation is to make her holy. It is a path to holiness. To be a wife and mother is difficult—a woman will suffer in this vocation. She will have the Cross in her life, and her relationship with her husband will not always be easy. But if they love each other, if they enter marriage because God wanted this and God blessed it, through His Cross they will be holy. And in this a couple will have peace. And if a woman marries for God, she will be open to the children God sends her. It will not matter how much money she has or how much patience she thinks she has for children or what she wants from life. Life will no longer be about her—this is especially true for a woman. To a true woman of God, life is not about her. Life is about others. Life is about God. If a woman does not serve like that, she will not be happy. But if she will give everything to Jesus, which the rich young man refused, (maybe not physically give away everything but if in her heart she does not cling to anything), and Jesus says, "No, I don't want you to have another husband. I love you. I want to be ALL for you, I want to be your Husband. I want for my children in the world to have YOU as their mother. Do you know what it means to be with Me?" Then she must receive this! She must trust in her First Love.

Each person needs to be that rich young man—but one needs to be different from him. When Jesus says, "Give away all and come to Me," a person needs to look at Jesus and then it will be very easy to do what He asks. If a man wants to give his entire life in order to make his beloved happy, any woman would want to be with him, would want to obey him. And that is Who Jesus is. He is that Man. He gave His whole life to give humanity happiness. He said, "Come to Me and receive all the love and mercy and patience you need." He cares about each person's body; He cares about each person's emotions, mind, and heart. He cares for all. And He will give a woman seeking His will that which will give the highest peace and joy. A woman must go to Him and not hold anything back. Each woman must ask, "What am I holding back in my heart?" She must search and ask, "What would I not want to give Him?" She must give Him that which she is holding for herself. A person must go to Jesus without anything in her hands and say, "Yes, maybe I am among people and things, but I am without anything. I have nothing. I am Yours. Tell me what You want. I am looking at Your Love. Help me answer You." And Jesus' Love will carry such an open heart. And in His Love, a woman will come to know His will.

God gave a woman ears, but they are also a sign of something inside of her. And her heart also has ears. And these ears must be open to His voice. There are many voices that will speak to a woman: the world, others, the devil. Who should she listen to? God gave a woman eyes. But also her heart has eyes. Where does she look? At things, people, herself, power, popularity? Each woman should ask, "What is my god?" And then give that 'god' to God and take Him as one's only possession instead. In her doing this, God will tell a woman what He wants with her life in His time and place. But she should wait for His answer. She should not grasp anything for herself.

I always wanted many children—a holy family—I always wanted an earthly husband. And it was very difficult for God to open my hands from holding onto my will. It was a good desire I had—a very holy Catholic family with 20 children or so. I said, "Jesus, I will adopt all children whom no one loves—just give me a holy husband." And one by one Jesus pulled each of my fingers back from clinging to my own will, and when He would get to the last finger my first one would clutch again. But, through His time and place He was able to show me His will. And He wanted me for Himself. He wanted for me to be your mother. He wanted me to be free and full of His Husbandly Love to love the world. He helped me to listen to His vocation. And I know now that I could never have such peace and joy and life with anyone else. Jesus created me for this vocation—to be His little wife on the Cross. I always desired Him, although I thought I desired an earthly husband. I did not know myself. But I did not create myself. He created me—He knew me better. And He eventually helped me discover who He created me to be.

A young woman must open her heart and listen to what Jesus wants for her life. Maybe Jesus will want for a given woman to be the wife and mother of someone here on earth—and in this she will listen to His voice through her husband. She will teach her husband to love God. She will love Jesus as a Child through her love for her children. Each time she holds her own children (if she will have them) that will be little Jesus that she is holding and loving. But maybe Jesus wants for a given woman to be His wife, for her to serve all His children. They are both very beautiful vocations. It is most important that a young woman waits and listens, that she does not take her will onto herself. God is different than we know and think. A young woman must listen to Him and to His vocation to her heart.

And so, how exactly does God reveal a vocation to a human heart? He speaks to a person through different situations, through a spiritual director, through the Church. He speaks through His word in the Bible and through His voice in one's heart. A person should not be afraid of what Jesus asks of her (like the rich young man had fear). Instead of fear, she simply should not look at herself, at her fear, at her thoughts, at her things, at her family—she should look at HIM! She should gaze at His look, for His glance can do all because it is a look full of Love.

This is the lesson to be learned: a woman must listen to God and obey. If He wants for her to have a husband, He will give her one in His Own time. But if Jesus does not want this, she should not take one herself, because it is not possible to live as a wife and husband without the grace of God. It is too hard. It is not possible. A marriage NEEDS His blessing. Amen.

Why the priesthood is not a vocation God gifts to Women

In light of this reflection on vocations, I want to touch here just for a moment on the question of why the priesthood is never one of the vocations that God gifts to women. This is a question often encountered in our modern world, and so I want to briefly explain why this vocation cannot fit with a feminine nature. As can be seen above, women are called to serve the Church through their varying vocations, yet they are never called to serve as priests. First of all, priests represent Christ on earth. Christ was male. Christ called the Church His Bride.

A female cannot (when things are properly ordered in accordance with natural law) marry a bride. Therefore, in order to remain faithful to the roles Jesus wanted priests to play, priests must be men. Sometimes, women claim to feel 'called' to the priesthood and attempt to justify the rightness of having women priests by their feelings. But, it must be understood that no one deserves the priesthood or enters into it because of a feeling. Even a man who feels a 'calling' to the priesthood must first be invited to this vocation by a bishop (who, tradition teaches, is guided by the Holy Spirit.) Therefore, feeling a 'calling' does not equal a 'right to ordination.'

Prevention of women to the priesthood is not the Church's way of keeping women out of any decision-making roles. In decision-making in the Church, all (including women) should be consulted. In the past, many women have greatly influenced the life and decisions of the Church, including Hildegard of Birgen, Bridget of Sweden, St. Theresa of Avila, St. Catherine of Siena, and even the writings of a simple, little saint—St. Teresa of Lisieux. The priest's role in the liturgy manifests a man's fatherhood, yet roles also exist in the church that manifest woman's motherhood. Often, women have excelled in prophesy, which can be used to nurture the faith of others as they act as spiritual directors, preachers, teachers, and mothers.

Women have a special aptitude for the contemplative life, and this is considered to be the highest vocation. Fr. Benedict Ashley, OP, writes that "the contemplative life directed towards (God) is superior to the active life directed towards this world."[1] Yet, Aquinas would argue that 'light that illumines is better than light which merely

---

[1] Ashely, Benedict M., *Justice in the Church* (Washington, D.C.: The Catholic University of America Press, 1996), p. 131.

shines.'[2] Therefore, consecrated female virgins who live a contemplative life but allow it to inspire and fill their actions are of those closest to God. Fr. Ashley explains:

> Vowed virgins in the Church, therefore, were Christians who had consecrated their entire life, including all their energy and intimacy of love which they were capable, to Christ with whom they hoped to live for all eternity on the Great Wedding Day. What was celebrated therefore was not a negative lack of earthly sexual experience, but the positive love of exclusive engagement to Christ.[3]

Just as priests represent Christ to the world, consecrated virgins represent Mary, a symbol of the new Eve, the Mother of Christ, and the Church herself. Men cannot do this. So, as women are excluded from the sacrament of priesthood, men are excluded from consecrated virginity in its full symbolic meaning. God made men and women different and called them to different things, but that does not mean that they are not equal in the dignity that their individual roles play. Why, then, is the priesthood considered a sacrament and consecrated virginity is not? This is because a sacrament is entered into for the purpose of conferring graces that help a person in the struggles of earthly life. But, consecrated virginity has nothing to do with the earthly life, but is a life of anticipation for eternal life.

Although women are not called to be priests, they are called to play an important role in the life of priests. First of all, just as Mary gave life

---

[2] Ashley, p. 133.

[3] Ashley, p. 139.

to Jesus the Son of God, so, too, mothers give life to priests. Pope John Paul, II says,

> "Behind this mission (of priesthood) there is the vocation received from God, but there is also hidden the great love of our mothers, just as behind the sacrifice of Christ in the Upper Room there was hidden the ineffable love of his mother. O how truly and yet how discretely is motherhood and thus womanhood present in the Sacrament of Holy Orders!"[4]

Priests relate to women throughout their lives. Some have sisters growing up. As they enter into the priesthood, they must come to have a deep understanding of all women as their sisters in Christ, mothers in Christ, and daughters in Christ. Women also aid priests in parishes and schools in the work they do. Women have a vital role to play in the Church's life—but it must be in accordance with their natural gifts of womanhood.

■ ■

To think about....

1. What do I keep to myself in my life? The rich young man clung to his riches and so he could not listen to Jesus. What do I cling to in my life?
2. How can I listen better to Jesus and His vocation for my life?

---

[4] Pope John Paul II, *Genius of Woman* (Washington, D.C.: United States Catholic Conference, Inc., 1997), p. 66.

3. When I encounter difficult things in life, where do I look for an answer? To Jesus' eyes *looking at me with Love* or somewhere else?

4. What kind of vocation do I feel God might be calling me to? How do I know that? (It is not only a feeling, it is something bigger.) If you don't know, don't worry –but begin to think about it.

Chapter 7

The Gift of Purity

Purity is a gift that God gave to woman. But although God gave women this very important gift, many times women do not use it. They make this gift of purity inside-out. God gave women the gift of purity in order to help men become close to God, and yet often women instead try to tempt men to be close to themselves. To understand how women misuse this gift of purity, at first a definition of purity must be given. What is purity? ***Purity does not mean 'the absence of man'*** *(which is often the definition accepted in today's world)*. ***In reality, purity is to be full of the presence of God.*** This does not mean to be with God. But to *be full of* something is different than to be *with* something. One can take a cup and place a spoon within it, but it is not full of a spoon. It can only be full of water, coffee, or something like that. In the same way, purity is not just living with God next to one's heart—having Him be part of one's life. Purity means to be soaked with God, full of Him in every part of one's being. This is what it means to be pure—to be one with and full of God.

This definition is important because people often think that purity means that a woman has no relationship with a man, or that she has not been close to a man. But purity is not only about one's body; purity is a state of heart. If a person has God, he is pure. God created a person's body to be totally united with one's soul, which is totally united with Him. That means that as God fills one's soul with His presence, one's body is also full of His presence in all of its actions. In this definition, a girl could be raped and remain very pure (it depends on her state of heart). But if her heart was with God during the violence she suffered, then she is full of God, she is pure. And nothing that another person has done to her body can take that. Jesus said, "*Do not worry about what people can do to your body. Worry about sin and what the devil can do to your soul.*" This is very important to know: to be pure means to have God soaked into the very heart of one's being.

A husband and wife have a very close relationship with each other. If a husband and wife join in sexual union, does this mean that they are not pure? No! They are very pure if their hearts are with God in their marital love, if their relationship is about God. If God is truly the center of their relationship, then in a man and his wife's sexual union they are simply obeying what God said to them in Genesis. If their relationship as a husband and wife is obedient to God—they want to give themselves to each other, they want to give life, they want to give love—then they actually grow in purity through their action of marital love. Pope John Paul II (in his *Theology of the Body*) created a new definition of Virginity. Virginity means the perfect union of body and soul with each other and with God. It means that one's body does not act out of sync with one's soul and its union with God. In this way, purity is a state of heart (if you remember the Catechism's definition of heart was the deepest part of the human body and soul). This is how Christopher West described the Pope's teaching (The italics are the Pope's actual words):

Every time that man and woman unite as one flesh, they are

tapping into God's original plan and they are meant to be renewing it.

"Man and woman uniting as one in the marital act return in that way to that union in humanity—'bone of my bone, flesh of my flesh' which allows them to recognize each other and like the first time call each other by name." In Genesis, Adam looks at Eve and says, "You are woman!" Eve looks at Adam and says, "You are man!" Even today, man and woman are called to discover each other's true identity in that marital embrace. *"This means that a marital embrace is reliving the original virginal value of man, which emerges from the mystery of his solitude before God."*

The Pope is saying here in some way, that a true marital act is not a loss of virginity, but it is a living of the truth of virginity. "The original, virginal value of man"—What is that? The Pope brings a deeper understanding of virginity to us. We think of virginity as, "A virgin has never had sex with anybody." **Virginity, as the Pope defines it, has to do with the integrity of the body and the soul.** That there is no rupture (or break) between the body and the soul. **Virginity means that the human being is untouched by the break between body and soul.** In the beginning remember that man and woman's bodies and souls were united perfectly. So when they became one body, they also became one spirit. **It was a spiritual love they were expressing in sexual union.** And so in this way they were confirming what it meant to be human. They were confirming in sexual union the dignity of the body. They were confirming the dignity of the person. The marital act was not the loss of anything. This was a gain. The loss of virginity in this deeper sense, comes with the dawn of sin when the body and the soul breaks—and now people usually experience sexual union not as an integrating experience (where body and soul are united) but in a disintegrating experience (where the body is ripped from the soul). And in this way sexual union becomes a loss of virginity—or we could say sexual union shows us how our virginity has been lost in sin (because usually people unite in body without uniting in soul and spirit). **The deeper meaning of virginity is the union of body and soul untouched by the break of sin. When man and woman unite in one flesh—A man and woman who have allowed Christ to transform their sexual desires—their experience of the marital act is not a loss, but they are slowly regaining their original union of body and soul. Sexual union (when transformed in Jesus) helps people become more united in body and soul—and therefore helps a person be more of a virgin!**

And so the marital act becomes a reliving of the original, virginal value of the human being. Virginity is man's solitude before God. It was when man stood as a body united with his soul before God. And the original unity returned to them because in sexual union Adam and Eve stood as one body and soul before God. And so in a sense, when Adam and Eve were united as one before God, they were brought back to their solitude –they were so one that they were seemingly one body and soul alone before God. And in that way it was a rediscovery of their virginity.

Mary was the purest woman who ever was: because she from the first moment of her life was full of God. All of her heart, emotions, thoughts, body, soul—ALL was fully united in and with God. She was totally united to God because she was without sin. What separates a soul from God? What separates a human heart from being totally full of God? Sin. For example: if there is a cup, it can be filled with water. But if something is taken and put in this cup full of water, the water falls out, goes out. Less water can be there because there is only a certain amount of space. The cup can be full of something: either water or a spoon or something else. This is how it is with the heart of a person. God created the human person to be full of Him. But when a person sins, he puts something else in his heart, so that he cannot receive all the love or presence of God that God desires for a soul. But Mary was without sin, so she was full of God. And for that reason she was pure.

Purity is something that can be read about in Genesis. The first sin of Eve was a sin against purity. What happened there? What happened in Paradise? God created Adam and Eve and He gave them Paradise. And He gave them all that they could ever want. They needed nothing—God always gave them all they needed. And that is how God created humanity to simply live—open and receiving from Him always. Just as a woman receives from her husband, so her husband would have received from God—that is how God created humanity to be. He wanted to provide everything for man and woman because they were His children. God said to His children Adam and Eve, "*Look. See that tree? Do not eat from that tree. Because I love you. I love you very very much. I do not want for you to have a problem. I do not want for you to worry about good and evil.*" He said, "*Let Me love you and give all that you need. Trust in Me.*" He knew what was the best for them.

But Eve did not trust God. The snake spoke to her and said, "*God does not want what is best for you, He wants something bad. You do not need God. Do you want to be God? Take this... Do not trust in your*

God, your Father." And she listened. That was her first problem. She listened to a voice other than her Father's. If the devil starts to tempt a person, he should not even listen.

What did Eve do when satan asked her this? She replied, *"Yes, maybe... I don't know..."* That was her second mistake: She spoke with the devil. So Eve's first mistake was to listen to the devil. Her second was to enter into a conversation with him.

I tell you now—the devil is many times smarter than any human. He was the very smartest angel. He was an angel –the very smartest: Lucifer. I say the smartest and not the wisest because wisdom is a gift of the Holy Spirit. Wisdom is a state of heart—to be wise means that one's hearts listens to God. Wisdom does not mean that I have a lot of knowledge or that I understand a lot of things and so I am wise. No, to be wise means that my heart always listens to God. And if I need something to say to someone God tells me what to say in that moment. But that knowledge and understanding is not mine—I do not have wisdom. I simply have the gift to be open and listen.

That is why wisdom is a gift of the Holy Spirit—it means that my heart is open and listens and God fills me. Wise people listen. They do not hold on to knowledge. So satan was smart—he had a very good mind. But he had pride and did not want to listen or serve. And he fell. And he wanted to take humanity with him. And so it is very important that when a person feels tempted that she never listen or speaks with the devil. He is smart in his tactics. Instead, one must remember she is a child of God and run to Him in trust... not always understanding, but instead obeying Him and trusting because He is her Father of Love.

And so the devil went to Eve and said, *"You don't want to serve, do you? You want to rule yourself, you want to decide?"* And she listened to him and she spoke with him. She was weak; she was a woman. Was this only her fault? No. Where was her husband during this? In her relationship with her husband, her husband was supposed to protect her. God had *entrusted* her to him. If in marriage a woman's body is no longer her own, if it is her husband's (for she has gifted it to him), if her whole being is gifted to him, then her husband has the responsibility to protect and care for that body and soul. It is not only his responsibility to protect and care for her physically by providing food, shelter, etc., but also spiritually in helping her listen to God's voice and protecting her from evil.

In marriage it is said that a wife needs to obey her husband, but her husband also has the responsibility to make her holy. So, it was not only Eve's fault that she fell into sin. Where was her husband who should have protected her from evil? And so she sinned. She decided, "*Ok. I will not listen to God and trust Him. I will listen to the devil.*" Every time the devil tempts a person, she has the decision, "*Whose voice will I listen to? The voice of my Father and God or the voice of the devil? This is my decision.*" It is so important to always listen to God. A tempted soul should say, "**Help me, Jesus.**"

Eve did not go to her husband and say, "*I can't do this alone, I have a temptation, I am weak. Help me.*" She did not say, "*God, I need You. Help me.*" She simply agreed to sin. If a person encounters a temptation, especially against purity, she needs to say, "*Jesus, help me. I am weak. I don't want to sin. I don't want to sin. I want to listen to you and serve You. Help!*" And He will help, I promise. And so that was Eve's sin. But it was not all her own fault. It was her fault, but her husband was culpable as well.

And so what happened after this? Eve went to her husband. She did not go to her husband to listen to him as she should have. She went to her husband to try to guide him, tell him what to do. In a marriage, the wife must listen to her husband, who is supposed to be listening to the Holy Spirit, and let him guide and protect her. But Eve turned this order—placed by God—inside out. She went to her husband to tell him what to do. This was not her place. She did not go to encourage him to listen to God or to pray with him about God's will. She went to tempt him to do evil. She said, "*Take and eat.*" And he listened! This was his fault.

A husband must remember that it is his place to lead and to help his wife to God, to holiness. So yes, she tempted him. But he allowed himself to be tempted. It was not only her fault. All was opposite from the order God had established. Suddenly, Eve—a woman—was like a man: she decided and ruled, tempted and controlled. And Adam—a man—was like a woman. He received the fruit in weakness instead of protecting her in strength. He didn't use the gift that God had given to him of reasonably thinking through the difficult situation presented to him. He simply said, "*Okay, I'll do whatever you want. I obey.*" And for that reason they fell. They sinned. They were no longer in union with God—full of God. Eve should have been looking at Adam, who should have been looking at God. But instead Eve was looking at her own desires in sin, and Adam was looking at her.

And yet this sad story of how impurity entered the world does not end on a hopeless note. Jesus lived perfect purity, and He gifts that to humanity on the Cross. All that was broken in man and woman's purity by original sin was healed by Jesus' incarnation, and especially by His perfection of Love shown by His total sacrifice on the Cross. For all of His life Jesus lived the perfect relationship with the Father—the sort of relationship God intended for

humankind from the beginning. For Jesus always focused on His Father. He always spoke of how He came not to do His own will, but only His Father's will. Adam and Eve had grasped at the forbidden fruit in the Garden of Eden. Jesus, *"though he was in the form of God, did not regard equality with God something to be grasped. Rather, he emptied himself, taking the form of a slave, coming in human likeness; and found human in appearance, he humbled himself, becoming obedient to death, even death on a cross."*[1]

Adam and Eve disobeyed. Jesus obeyed unto DEATH! Adam and Eve ate the fruit of the forbidden tree and thus entered darkness and had to be thrown from the Garden. Jesus willingly entered the Garden to suffer and pray. He was invited back into that Garden to redeem the sin which had occurred there. And Jesus also in obedience had to eat the fruit of a tree—the horrific fruit of the Cross. This fruit was not pleasing to Jesus' eye or taste (as the 'forbidden fruit' had been to Adam and Eve), for it was a symbol of everything which hurt His Father, Whom He dearly loved. And yet in obedience, He had to 'drink His cup.'

Jesus' Love had to conquer all sin and death let into the world by Adam and Eve's sin. And in His surrender, in His Fiat, in His trust in His Father for everything He needed (a trust that was not even broken by what seemed to be His Father's abandonment on the Cross), He made all things new. When a woman comes to Jesus on the Cross, He can heal her broken purity. Where Eve said, "Take and Eat" to her husband, giving sin to humanity, Jesus says "Take and Eat" to humanity, offering His very body as a remedy to that sin. This purification of womanhood from Jesus on the Cross gives woman once again the possibility of being a great instrument of

---

[1] Phil 2:6-8.

God's pure and holy love in the world.

God gave woman the gift of being a 'temptress,' in that women are attractive to men. And that attractiveness has an influence over them. **But God gave woman the gift of being attractive—'a holy temptress' so to speak, so that she could tempt men to love God.** It is true, man likes woman. This is not bad. God created woman as a gift for man. This is not amazing or bad. But woman has a responsibility as man's gift to tempt him to be holy and to love God. Woman has a gift to teach man: she shows through example that the sort of relationship she has with man is the sort of relationship man should have with God. And so she teaches him. One could say that she tempts him to be holy and with God. If a man is in love with a woman, she has a sort of power over him. Maybe he does not say, "Oh, she is so beautiful. I want to do all she says." But if she is pure and holy then a woman can tempt the man to do all she wants to make him holy.

So the first sin was opposite than the order and plan of God. God created woman to be a temptress of man, but in order to tempt man (to attract man) to fall in love with Himself. But woman tempted man to the devil—to sin—to death. Woman has the gift to give life. What does it mean to give life? It is to give God, for God is life. So if woman tempts man to God, she gives him life because God is the source of all Life. If a woman tempts a man to be holy, he receives the Holy Spirit— the presence of God deep within himself, and he is holy. He has a possibility for eternal life. But if she tempts him to sin, she is not living her responsibility to give life. It is opposite than what she was created to do. In tempting man to sin, she is receiving and giving death, sin— not life. In that garden, Eve received sin from the devil and gave sin to humanity. It was not her function. God created her to receive life from Him and to give it to humanity. And she changed this inside out—she turned from God to the devil—and she received sin and death from him and gave that to humanity.

And so thankfully humanity has the gift of Mary. She is the Church's New Eve. Why is She called the New Eve? It is because She received life from God which gave humanity eternal life. Eve listened to the devil. Maria listened to God. Eve obeyed the devil. Maria obeyed God. Maria said, *"I am the servant of the Lord. I will do all what You want, God. Fiat. Yes! I want to receive from You."* Eve said, *"I will not be your servant, and I will not even be your daughter. I do not want this relationship with You."* Eve was proud. God gave her the possibility to be His child—she was His daughter, He cared for her as a daughter— He gave her all she needed. God was like a mother when she has a child who does not know what is good and bad—it did not matter if Adam and Eve knew good or evil because God knew and cared for them. God gave all they needed, and they did not need to understand or know.

God decided for them what was dangerous and what was good. That is the kind of relationship Eve had with God. Eve was not a daughter in the exact same way that we can be daughters of God after Jesus came. Jesus changed our relationship with God totally. But Adam and Eve's relationship with God was like a child's with his parent. Yet, after Eve listened to the devil and disobeyed God, she was no longer a daughter of God; she separated herself from Him. She could no longer live in His 'womb;' she had chosen to step out of a love relationship with Him. And He had to allow her to go, even if it broke His Heart, because she was free.

And yet Mary changed all this in Her Fiat. She was not proud and did not try to 'shake' God out of her life. She not only recognized her place as God's child, but She also lowered herself to be His slave. And in her humility and docility She was able to receive our salvation (Jesus) and birth Him to the world. Mary did not say, "I want to be your daughter." She said, *"I want to be your servant."* Her humility was amazing. Her obedience was amazing. Eve tempted humanity to sin. Mary, the Mother of God, our Mother (you can say) tempted humanity to God. Mary has appeared many times on earth over many years. And each time She did this, people never clung to Mary Herself. Every time She has come to earth She has said what she said in Cana when there was no wine and they did not know what to do. There She said to the servants, *"Do whatever my Son tells you. Listen to and obey my Son."* And from that time until now each time She appears She says, *"Listen to my Son. Do not look at me, look at Him. Do not love me, love Him. Go to Him."* She tempts us to be holy, to go to God, to love God.

Mary was the most pure virgin, for Her heart was always fully possessed by God's Love. Mary's purity (Her being possessed by the Holy Spirit and Love of God) is witnessed to in a special way if one looks again at St. John's Gospel account of the wedding at Cana. Here can be seen Mary's heart completely surrendered and dependent on Her Lover for all. Mary saw a need. She did not go to anyone else but Her Beloved for help. She did not seek an answer on Her own but followed the Holy Spirit guiding within Her to ask Her Son and Her Spouse, Christ for help. (For Christ, as God, was also the Spouse of Mary's Heart.)

Mary went to Jesus, her Heart's only Love, and trustingly asked for help. Mary's focus was on the Heart of Jesus, and She had great faith in His Heart. She trusted His Heart's Love. Her chaste heart, full of the Love of God, purely understood God's will and She obeyed His will by requesting Her Son's help. Her Love was so pure that it cut through all, keeping Her undisturbed by Her Son's question, '*Woman, how does your concern affect me? My hour has not yet come,*'[2] focusing on the Trinitarian Love pressing Her to speak. She trusted, maybe not understanding His words, but trusted in His Love. Her faith was perfect through perfect Love. Perhaps it was not yet "His time" when Jesus spoke these words to His mother. And yet Her action of trust in Him unlocked, in a way, His Heart so that it suddenly was "His time." Maybe in that moment He truly was asking, "*Do you know how your request, your concern, is affecting me? If you ask such things in faith, trust and Love, it will bring 'My hour'.*"

The 'fullness of time' happened for the first time when Mary said, "Yes, Fiat," to the angel. With Her surrender to God's will, our Savior could come to dwell on earth within Her womb. Her first "Yes" ushered in the 'fullness of time,' and now here at Cana Her same 'Yes,' Her same trust in the Father, was a resting place creating the atmosphere of trust needed for 'Jesus' time' to unfold. Her action of trust was an action of purity, for She was totally possessed with the presence of Love, of the Holy Spirit, in Her request to Her Son.

In Dante's *Divine Comedy*, there is a very beautiful example of woman being a good temptress of man to fall in love with God. There was a woman in this book named Beatrice. She was very beautiful, and Dante fell in love with her. He could only look at her beauty— "Beatrice, My Beatrice!" his heart would beat. But she looked at God. She was in heaven. She did not look at him. She looked at God. And Dante looked at her and said, "Oh, look, look! How beautiful!" And he looked at her legs and fingernails, at everything—and he found her eyes and said, "Where do her eyes look? They look at something.

---

[2] John 2:4.

Where is her glance? It is so beautiful!" And so he looked and followed her glance and found that she was looking at God. When he followed her glance to God his glance became fixed on the beauty and wonder of God. He almost forgot about her. He did not stand facing her looking at her and she looking at him with God somewhere around them. No, she looked at God and he followed her eyes to God and then they stood next to each other and looked together on God. This is an example of the work entrusted to women. A woman must always live a life looking at God and in this she will tempt man to look at God.

It is important for a woman to keep and use the purity of her eyes. Eyes are a very powerful tool to help draw men to God. When a man is looking at a woman's eyes, she has a decision to draw him to God or to draw him to herself for herself. If a woman—who has a very pure heart—looks back into his eyes, it speaks something very loud to a man. I remember being mortified in high school when I went out one night with my friends and as we were sitting around playing cards (and they were drinking beer) one burst out across the table at me, "Mary, you remind me of one of those girls right out of the Bible! There is just something so innocent and pure about you!"

Being in high school I was not really thrilled about being considered the 'pure one' of the group, although in my heart (torn between a great love for God and a desire to be cool and included) I had to rejoice that this kid saw a small piece of God in me. A woman must be like Beatrice and Mary. She should be constantly looking at God in her heart and in that the man who looks at her would say, "Her eyes are glowing with a heavenly beauty. Where are her eyes looking?" Women have a huge possibility to tempt men to God. Women have a huge possibility to give eternal life to men. And this is because God created them to be a gift to men. Women must use that gift. It is very important that women live as temptresses as Jesus wants, as God wants—to help men be holy.

It is most important for a woman's heart to be centered on God—for sin takes place in the heart before it takes place in the body. Jesus said, *"You have heard that it was said, 'You shall not commit adultery.' But I say to you, everyone who looks at a woman with lust has already committed adultery with her in his heart"* (Mt 5:27-8). So the old law says, 'You shall not have sex with someone who is not your wife.' But Jesus says, "If you look at someone and want that in your heart, it is already a mortal sin.'" A woman must be careful to guard her heart from sin—in that way she will not lead others into sin. This is why it is important for a woman to pray in general—because prayer helps her heart to always be with God. If her heart is with God, people will see it. And then she will not have to worry about how she sits or what she wears because she will naturally sit and dress in a pure way. A person's actions in body reflect what is in one's heart. If one's heart is somewhere bad, it is also very clear through one's body. A woman's heart needs to want only God—not pleasure for herself, or just pleasure for others. Life should not be centered on pleasure but instead centered on God's Love. God gives a person other people to love, but one has to love as He wants.

Where does the beauty of woman come from? It is from God's special gift to her of Love. If the heart of a person is with God, then it is visible throughout her entire body. This is because God's presence is Love and Beauty Itself. And so when God lives fully in a woman open to His Love, His presence makes her beautiful. In Bosnia, the Blessed Mother has appeared daily to seven children (who are now adults) from 1980 until the present. When the apparitions began, the children were especially amazed at the Blessed Mother's beauty, for they had never seen anyone even as close to being as beautiful as she was. And so one day they asked her, "Why are you so beautiful?" The Blessed Mother smiled and answered, *"I am beautiful because I love. If a person loves, he is full of God and God's beauty shines from him."* God is beauty. He created mountains, flowers, people—He is Beauty Itself.

So if Beauty Himself lives in a woman, she will be beautiful. Often, there are people who the world might say are 'beautiful' (models, for example), and yet if sin is inside of them, they have no light—their natural 'beauty' is distorted. But when a person, who is not even that beautiful in the world's standards, is full of the beauty and love of Jesus, then he suddenly is really beautiful and everyone wants to be close to him. Mother Teresa is a good example of this. She did not wear the most 'fashionable' clothes (for she was in a habit) and was not considered beautiful by worldly standards—but she was full of Jesus and so people were attracted to her. People just wanted to be with her because they found their God in her. A woman must search for beauty through love. The world says, "Women need lots of make-up or in-style clothes to be beautiful." But that is a mask. God gives a woman beauty in herself—in how He created her with His Love. A woman should not hide His beauty. If a woman holds God in her heart, she will show God to the world—her presence will proclaim His beauty, not her own. A woman should be like God created her to be. She must believe that she is very beautiful, and she must protect and treasure her beauty for God and for her future husband someday (if she will be called to marriage.)

A woman's body is a gift. God wants for a woman to use this gift of her body to help people, to help man. A woman's body should not be used to make herself 'feel good' or to make man 'feel good.' A body was not given for this purpose—the gift of one's body is much deeper than this. If two people love each other, they can show this love to each other through appropriate gestures of their body, but they must be very careful in guarding such actions in the purity of God's presence between them. St. Francis de Sales, in his *Treatise on the Love of God*, explains how powerful even one kiss between two people in love can be. He says that in a kiss one person is saying to another, *"I want to pour my soul into your heart."* He writes, *"And thus one mouth is applied to another in kissing to testify that we would desire to pour out one soul into the other, to unite them reciprocally in a perfect union."*[3]

And so although the gesture of a kiss can be an appropriate sign of affection in some circumstances, it needs to be centered in God and be an expression of something deep within a person. For St. Francis de Sales writes that a kiss is "a lively mark of the union of hearts."[4] When two people are in love they must ask themselves, *"Does this action bring my soul closer to God?"* True Love expressed appropriately always brings two people closer to God, for true Love expressed in the body is always done in union with God. As soon as a woman is shamed about her body's expressions of love, it is a sign that her body has partaken in an action not in union with her soul or God's plan of Love for humanity.

In the Garden of Eden, Adam and Eve were naked without shame.

---

[3] St. Francis de Sales, translated by Dom Henry Benedict Mackey, O.S.B., *Treatise on the Love of God* (Rockford, Illinois: Tan Books and Publishers, Inc., 1997), p. 38.

[4] St. Francis de Sales, p. 38.

After they sinned, they were embarrassed of their bodies and wanted to cover them (lest they be used merely as instruments of pleasure). Yet Jesus on the Cross was naked and abused to redeem both a person's body and soul, and to help a person enter into again the purpose for which God created him. And so in Jesus, man and woman can once again use their bodies to express love in holy and appropriate ways without shame.

Ephesians 5:1-5 speaks clearly about how one should imitate God in all one's actions, especially those having to do with expressing love to another human being. St. Paul clearly states, *"So be imitators of God, as beloved children, and live in love, as Christ loved us and handed himself over for us as a sacrificial offering to God for a fragrant aroma. Immorality or an impurity or greed must not even be mentioned among you, as is fitting among holy ones, no obscenity or silly or suggestive talk, which is out of place, but instead, thanksgiving. Be sure of this, that no immoral or impure or greedy person, that is, an idolater, has any inheritance in the kingdom of Christ and of God."*

This is clear. A woman must strive to imitate God. He created woman in His image, and so she needs to live as He would live—as His beloved child. In questions of expressing love to a man, a woman must ask the question, *"Is this something I would do knowing that God, my Father, is watching?"* There are things that a woman would be embarrassed to do in front of her Father. And as God's beloved child, He is always with her. And so a woman should live remembering that her Father sees all. She must live in Love as Jesus lived Love. She must express her Love as Jesus expressed His Love on the Cross—in purity and seeking to be a gift that brings her beloved closer to his Father. A woman should live and love like Jesus. He *'handed himself over for us as a sacrificial offering to God for a fragrant aroma.'* He gave Himself as a sacrifice to give humanity holiness. He opens man's and woman's purity on the Cross. He is naked.

In paradise, before they fell into sin, it is said that *'the man and his wife were naked, yet they felt no shame'* (Gen. 2:25). They felt no shame because there was no reason why they should have been embarrassed in their nakedness. Man and woman simply had their bodies that God gave them—full of His Love—and they gave these bodies to each other in union with their souls in accordance with God's plan (as He commanded them to do, saying *"Be fruitful and multiply..."*). On the Cross, Jesus gave back to man and woman this original innocence. He opened and purified all that was lost in sin. When man and woman share love purified by Christ, then they have a fragrant aroma. If their hearts are with God and they do not want or do impure things (things empty of God's presence), then this is visible to people—like a fragrant aroma. A man's and woman's presence with God itself says to the world, *"Impure things are really bad. They do not make a person happy. They are never beneficial to a human heart."* Simply by living God's plan for pure Love, a man and woman can proclaim His greatness in the world and bring Him great glory.

God created woman free, but He created her free so that she could freely choose to Love Him. A woman is only truly free when she uses her freedom to choose His Love. Any other choice locks a woman from God, and therefore locks her from herself—for a woman is only truly herself when God possesses her. And so, in order to be truly pure—full of the presence of God—a woman must be like a little child, resting in His bosom. Jesus said, *"Unless you become like little children you cannot enter the kingdom of God.*"[5] This is because children see truth. Children are trusting. Children are obedient. Children forgive and simply love. In embracing the gift of littleness, a woman can grow in purity. For littleness is humility—the truth of who she is before God. When a woman lives littleness, she has a docile heart in the hands of God; she trusts Him; she lives as if she is not her own. The more a woman allows Jesus to live in her,

> see in her,
> hear in her,
> think in her,
> speak in her,
> pray in her,
> rest in her,
> act in her … the purer she will become.

A woman needs to guard her purity of heart through silence and Love. She must not allow her heart to fall into the trap of watching too much TV (even the news), being consumed by shopping, or involved in needless conversations. For everything that does not help unite a soul with God separates her from Him. A woman should strive to be as simple as a child. A woman needs a certain amount of silence to keep her union—her 'communion' (and communication)—with God. Only with such a heart, centered in her Father's Heart, will she be able to readily discern what is good and evil, what is pure and impure, in the world around her. The more she dwells in Jesus' Love, the easier she will see the impurity of her own. Each time she receives the

---

[5] Matthew 18:3.

Eucharist, she must strive to let go of everything in her life and to simply allow Jesus' body and Heart to enter, fill, and transform hers.

In her receiving the Eucharist, it is like she is having a blood transfusion, allowing His blood to physically live in her, beat in her heart. When she goes to Communion, when she partakes of His Eucharistic sacrifice of Calvary with Him, she is filled physically with His Body, which is in perfect union with His soul dwelling in perfect union with His Father. In this, she is a treasurer of Jesus' Body and Soul—a chalice of His life-giving Blood. And **all she must do when she leaves Mass, is strive to live worthy of such a gift.** She must strive to open herself fully and allow Jesus to live within her, keeping her body and soul always united as one with the Father. And when she focuses on God and His Love, she naturally opens to receive this Love, to hear His Love, to be receive and be filled with this Love—and, in this, she becomes pure.

Jesus' Love must take the first place in a woman's life—not her love of people or the world or even her love of Him. But Jesus' Love must be the center of her life. A woman must allow Jesus' Love to live incarnated within her. She should watch for and listen to His Love ever present in every moment of her life, calling souls, creating life, giving Love. She must allow Him to conform her heart to His Own. This is something that can be easily done as she simply allows His Love to rule and guide every part of her life. A woman should lay down her mind, her emotions, and her actions into Jesus' arms of Love and simply rest with Him there. She should allow her life to always truly be a song, a worship and adoration of His Heart and Love crucified by simply remaining resting in Him and in allowing Him to live in her.

Some practical notes on purity

-*Men are weak in body, women are weak in heart...*

So, how can women help men to be holy? Men are very weak physically. In general, men are very strong in the way that their bodies are built, but about sexual things they are very weak in the physical realm. Men are easily opened in a physical way, and once their desire for sexual union is aroused, it is very difficult for them to refrain from completing the act. Women are not like this as much. They are not as easily opened in a physical way to want sexual union. A woman may desire such a union because she craves closeness with a man, but it is not like his physical urge that is difficult to control.

If a woman is physically intimate with a man and they find themselves in an inappropriate expression of love, she can very easily leave that situation, while a man has a more difficult time just stopping before his body completes the sexual act. And so a woman must see, respect, and help men as her brothers in this physical weakness. Women must help men to be pure. Both men and women fell into sin. Both men and women are sinners. Sin made humanity weak—very weak. If humanity was totally filled with God (and kept itself away from sin), then it would be very strong, for God's strength would fill it. But the sad reality is that both men and women do have sin in their hearts. That is a place without God. And, therefore, men and women are weak in these places of sin because God created them to be with Him always, and these spots are empty of His presence. And so women MUST help men be pure. Women must protect men from temptations physically. They must watch how they dress, what they say, what gestures they use, so that they do not open a man physically in such a way that he is tempted to desire completion of the sexual act. And if a woman sees that her physical relationship with a man is going too far, she must separate herself from him in order to avoid sin.

It is easier in the midst of a rush of emotions and bodily urges for women to remember such things than for men. But just as a man is weak in his bodily desires, a woman's heart is very weak when it comes to relationships with men. A woman's heart is easily opened to desire emotional love. And so men MUST protect women from emotional temptations. A man must be careful with a woman's heart and not play emotionally with her. Just as a woman must strive to protect a man's purity in body, a man must strive to protect a woman's heart. When a man and a woman are starting a relationship, the man should remember, "*I have to be careful, I don't want to say something so that she thinks I will love her more than I do.*"

When a woman loves, she wants to open her heart and speak everything about herself and to share every mystery and secret of her heart. She can share something physical with a man too, but her desire is to share her heart. A man must remind her (as is appropriate to the stage of their relationship), "*Don't tell me that yet. Be careful with your heart. Close that corner of your heart. Don't open that. That is something only for your husband. If I will be your husband someday then you can tell me that.*" So a man must protect the heart of a woman because she is very weak emotionally. But a woman must protect a man through keeping purity in her clothing, words, body, and gestures. Ultimately, if two people keep God as the center of their relationship, then He will keep their expressions of love appropriate and full of His purity.

~*Modesty in dress, action and words*

How can a woman be pure in dress, action, and words? Purity is to be full of God. And so when a man looks at a woman, he needs to be reminded of God. If a man sees too much of a woman's body, then he will think about her body. A woman has to be a hundred times more careful then about how she thinks about her clothing. Clothing says a lot. If a man sees too much of a woman's leg, if he sees too much skin, if a woman has a shirt that is open, a man can be tempted to focus on a woman's body and not on her heart. He can be tempted to desire her body for himself instead of focusing on giving himself in love for her. Because of sin, humanity is weak. And so even if it is true that the body of a woman in itself is not bad—it is a huge gift from God for man through marriage—a woman must respect the fallen nature of man and help him through dressing modestly so as to not lead him into sin.

The body of a woman is a gift. It is very beautiful. But a woman must save that gift. A person must save things that have big worth and beauty, things that are full of God, so that they will not be abused. A woman's body is like a temple of the Holy Spirit. In Genesis, it is written that God created man and woman and gave His Own breath as their life. The body is like a chapel –physically the Holy Spirit is there. And so a woman must save and treasure the gift of her body. She must protect it. She must respect it as the greatest tool she has to give her love (and God's love through her) to her husband. If a woman is not called to marriage, then she must keep the gift of her body as a treasure for her beloved Spouse Jesus alone. And the way a woman dresses and the actions she expresses should reflect the fundamental sacredness of her body given by God to be used as an instrument to bring man to closer to his Father in heaven.

A woman's words must also be very pure, instruments full of God's presence which lead men to God. Words are like capsules that gift a spirit to the listener. If a woman speaks words in love (even simple words used in ordinary life), then such words can draw a man closer to God. But if a woman speaks words with a selfish motive, then such words do not draw a man closer to God. A woman must be careful of her words, for if a woman is very beautiful to a man, he listens to her.

It is very important that a woman uses this gift to help her brothers be holy. Jesus says in the Gospel of Matthew, *"I tell you, on the day of judgment people will render an account for every careless word they speak"* (Matthew 12:36). Every word is important. A woman can play with words to tempt men. One's voice is not something only for the ears, but when a baby is little he needs a sweet, gentle voice as a form of touch. If words can be a form of touch for a child, they can also be for men. A woman must question herself, "How am I speaking to men? Why am I speaking this way? What am I speaking to them?"

St. Paul says clearly, *"Immorality or an impurity or greed must not even be mentioned among you, as is fitting among holy ones, no obscenity or silly or suggestive talk, which is out of place, but instead, thanksgiving."* A woman should not say words that are obscene, silly or suggestive. A woman's speech should lead others to thank God, to praise Him. St. Paul writes, *"Be filled with the Spirit, addressing one another in psalms and hymns and spiritual songs, singing and playing to the Lord in your hearts, giving thanks always and for everything in the name of our Lord Jesus Christ to God the Father"* (Ephesians 5:18-20).

A woman should speak of God's miracles, of His Love, of His life, of *"whatever is true, whatever is honorable, whatever is just, whatever is pure, whatever is lovely, whatever is gracious, if there is any excellence and if there is anything worthy of praise..."* (Phil 4:8). Each word a woman speaks is very important. And so she must be careful to always speak in a pure way, with words full of God's life-giving presence.

The body and its gestures speak very loudly. In the mission in Russia where I served, there was a priest who began Pantomime Theatre youth group. This group performed Theatre without words—instead acting and speaking only through the body's gestures. Silent gesture can be amazingly powerful in communicating. Often, the Gospel acted out in such a way moved people to tears. It was much stronger in touching hearts than the spoken word. The body's gestures can speak many times louder than words. If a person looks sad, but says he is happy, no one will believe him. His body speaks of sadness louder than his words can claim happiness.

Sometimes, one's body speaks even when he does not know it. How does a person sit? How does he hold himself? What is he doing with his hands? How is his face?—It all speaks. And so a woman must reflect on what she wants to say to men through her gestures. How a woman sits when she is with them can speak loudly. One gesture might mean nothing for a woman, but it could speak something to a man. And so a woman must be aware of the gestures she uses with men as much as she is aware of what words she chooses. A woman must treat men as her brothers by being modest and respectful of their weaknesses. Men are not bad. They are very beautiful gifts for women. But a woman needs to treasure the gift of men in her life by striving to help them be holy.

~Smoking, drunkenness, (abusive drugs) and overeating

A woman must protect her body like a temple of the Holy Spirit. She should not abuse tobacco, drugs, alcohol, or food. Such actions are not pure, for they are not actions of the body which unite a woman's soul with God. They seek pleasure at the risk of killing one's body. The Catechism states on this matter:

> The virtue of temperance disposes us to avoid every kind of excess: the abuse of food, alcohol, tobacco, or medicine. Those incur grave guilt who, by drunkenness or a love of speed, endanger their own and other's safety on the road, at sea or in the air. (2290)

A woman should not search pleasure for herself. Often, this quest for pleasure is the underlying source of the abuse of drugs, alcohol, tobacco (from these substances they seek a 'feeling' of pleasure) and food (women often have problems either searching for pleasure in food, or in not eating so that their bodies are more 'attractive' and they can have more pleasure with men). If every woman would respect her body as God wanted desired, she would not have to search for pleasure because God Himself would fill her and give all she needs, more than human pleasure.

It is important to emphasize here that pleasure in itself is not evil. God created things so that humanity would take pleasure in them. Why would He create a rose with a beautiful smell if He did not want for people to take pleasure in that smell, in its beauty? Why would He create a sunset if He did not want for people to rejoice with Him in the pleasure of its sight? But there is a difference between pleasure that gives life and pleasure that takes life. A woman's soul was created to receive, protect, nurture and gift life—and this includes her own life. She must receive the gift of her own life from God, nurture this life (she has to have a gift to be a gift), protect her own life (by not abusing her body through abuse of tobacco, alcohol, drugs, or food—in other words, by not doing anything that could harm her life directly) so that she can gift this life to the world. Seeking pleasure at the risk of harming life (as smoking, excess drinking, overeating, etc., does) separates the body's action from the soul's purpose for life (which is to be in union with God).

Anything that separates one's body's actions from the soul's purpose for existence (which is to give life and love) is not pure. It cannot be said that all smokers, drinkers, or overeaters are huge sinners going to hell. No human can judge another person's salvation. And such matters are left up to one's own conscience before the light of God. In order for something to be a sin, three things are needed:

1.) the action must be evil in itself;
2.) the person must know it is wrong;
3.) and the person must freely choose to do it anyway.

There are situations where these three things do not apply. For example, someone who has smoked for 40 years and then finds out it is wrong cannot be really considered 'free' to stop smoking. Although it is very laudable if they choose to do this, some situations make a person truly addicted in a way that reduces their freedom in the matter. Another example would be some people with eating disorders. Although it is inherently wrong to overeat, a person with an eating disorder has an eating sickness and sometimes is not culpable for her disordered action. Most important here is to remember (and to strive to live) the principle that a woman's body's actions should always coincide with her soul's attempt at union with God and His plan for her. A woman is a small little temple, a church, a chapel of the Holy Spirit. And so she should treat her body with the respect that her dignity demands. St Paul writes, *"Do you not know that your body is a temple of the Holy Spirit within you, whom you have from God, and that you are not your own? For you have been purchased at a price. Therefore, glorify God in your body"* (1 Corinthians 6:19-20).

The disorder of homosexuality

We spoke about purity especially when it comes to man-woman relationships. But in today's world there also is a big problem with homosexuality—lesbianism—this is directly against the plan of God, against how God created humans to live with each other. God did not create Adam and Adam, or Eve and Eve. He created man to be with woman. In today's world, there is a crisis in the family. Often, fathers and mothers are not very good. At times, problems arise between brothers and sisters, and sometimes there is even sexual abuse inside of the family. Men and women are sinners—the world is impure. And so many times men wound women. Women need love, like babies. And if women do not receive the love they need from men, many times they search for that from other women. (This is also true for men – they are wounded by women and therefore become homosexual—but I am specifically focusing here on women).

I remember working once with a poor woman who had been born

into a satanic family and from infancy she was severely sexually abused in occult activity. When she went to Protestant pastors or psychologists for help, they abused her as well. The priest who brought her to me and asked me to befriend and help her was literally the only male in her life who had never abused her. And so she was a lesbian. Her woundedness made her that way. We spent years introducing her to the faith and explaining why the Church taught what it did, and before she died she was received into the Catholic Church. She had finally found peace and joy in the truthful teachings of Jesus Christ.

Women have the gift of loving and being delicate and so often women who have not received the love from men that they crave search for this kind of love from women. But this is not the proper order of God. There is a difference between friendship and sickness, which is what lesbianism is. God wants for women to have friends, to have sisterly relationships, and He wants for women to love each other. But if a woman searches to receive something from another woman that she was created to only receive from a man, than that is a sickness. The cause of such behavior may be understandable because of her wound—but it is still a sin. And if the woman knows about this being a sin, and she freely chooses to embrace such a lifestyle anyway, she commits a big, mortal sin. If a woman has a problem with men (and she fears them and therefore has the temptation to go to women), she must go to Jesus. He will heal and open her.

Feminine friendship is so important to a woman. Such a thing is beautiful as long as it remains ordered to God's plan. In the Bible, we see beautiful examples of feminine friendship—especially in the friendship of Mary and Elizabeth. They are very close. They helped each other. They were so close that Jesus from Mary's womb baptized

John in Elizabeth's womb. But how did they live that friendship? How did they express that friendship? They did it purely as women, and they never sought to take a man's place. There was such a problem in Eden when woman tried to be man and man tried to be woman. It was the great fall of original sin. And sin is not only about one person. It is amazing how far one sin can go.

Original sin changed the entire course of history. But holiness can also go that far. The Salvation Jesus won for us on the Cross reached throughout all time to help all people. And if one, two, three people begin to live holiness reflecting Jesus', that also begins to affect many, many people. So women desperately need to be pure (purity meaning full of God's presence and Love). It is very important for women to remain faithful to whom God created them to be and how He created them to relate to each other.

When a woman is wounded in her relationships, it is so important that she goes to Jesus on the Cross and asks Him to heal her. Jesus gathered many women together around Him at the foot of the Cross. It is there that He won grace for feminine friendships to be rightly ordered and to bloom in deep, holy, pure love. And by a woman going to Jesus, His Manly Love will open her femininity and transform her many wounds and sicknesses. On the Cross, Jesus gave Mary to each woman as her Mother. May She be woman's guide as to how she can grow in feminine friendship and ordered, authentic Love in all of her actions and desires.

St. Maria Goretti

Most Catholics have heard about St. Maria Goretti. She was a very young girl in Italy. Her family was very poor. And one day a young man who worked on her father's farm wanted to rape her. Maria loved purity so greatly that she fought with this young man, and he in anger took a knife and stabbed her because she would not agree to allow him to rape her. Maria eventually died from her stab-wounds. She was a martyr, someone willing to give her life for purity. And yet before her death Maria forgave her attacker and gave her suffering as a sacrifice to convert that young man. And he eventually did convert.

Maria is a beautiful, courageous model for all women. She loved her purity so greatly, she treasured this gift so greatly, that she protected it unto death. She could have agreed with this man, and she would not have died. But she so loved the gift of her purity that she was willing to fight for it unto death. Every woman can pray to her when she has temptations. Even the purest of people have temptations because the devil wants to make humanity sin in purity, for that is a place where a person is deeply united with God. God allows such temptations so that people can grow in purity and become stronger as they continually choose Him.

At her canonization, Pope Pius XII said about her, *"Not all of us are expected to die a martyr's death, but we are all called to the pursuit of Christian virtue. This demands strength of character though it may not match that of this innocent girl. Still, a constant, persistent, and relentless effort is asked of us right up to the moment of our death."* St. Maria Goretti, pray for us.

■ ■

To think about...

1. Concretely, how you as a woman can grow in purity—in body, intention, speech, or heart?
2. How can I live more deeply united as one with Jesus in the Eucharist and after I leave Mass on a day-to-day basis?
3. How is Jesus asking me to grow in a love relationship with Him?

Chapter 8

Woman and the Cross, The Eucharist and Prayer

This is the most important chapter of this book, for it has to do with the deepest part of a woman's life—woman's relationship with Jesus' Own Heart in the Eucharist, woman's relationship with Jesus' sacrifice on the Cross, and woman's relationship with Christ in prayer. I invite the reader as we begin to take a Cross in one's hands and to look at Jesus on the Cross. The mystery of salvation is in this Cross. It is through this Cross that all that Adam and Eve ruined through sin (and all that humanity continues to destroy through sin) is transformed. For in original sin God's original plan for man and woman was mixed up. Eve was like a man—she did not listen to Adam, she listened to the devil. She took and led their relationship and said, "Adam, take this." And Adam did not listen to God as he was supposed to do. Instead he focused solely on Eve and obeyed her. This was all backwards from God's original plan.

Purity is especially a gift of woman. She was created to be full of God and to gift His life in fullness to others. Yet, Eve took sin on herself and in Eve's sin, the gift of purity was wounded—her body was separated from her soul and God's will and Love for her life. The Cross is where Jesus repaired that wound in man and woman's relationship (caused by original sin). On the Cross, Jesus opened and healed both woman and man, teaching them the truth of who they were created to be. Here Jesus gave both man and woman the possibility to have purity again. On the Cross Jesus took that first sin upon Himself and made it possible for humanity to receive the purity of the fullness of God's presence and Love and to allow this Love to dwell in their hearts. In Baptism, Jesus draws a human soul into the Cross and one's sin stays there. And after carrying a baptized Christian through His Cross, Christ continues to carry the soul through His resurrection with Him. It is in the Cross that humanity is renewed. And this is why the Cross is every Christian's hope.

Even the Blessed Mother finds Her source of purity in the Cross. How could this be so? How could She be born without sin if Jesus had not yet suffered to redeem sin? God does not live in time. God lives in eternity. Yes, Mary was born and only years later did an angel come to her to ask if she would be mother of Jesus. And it was 33 years after this that Her Son died on the Cross to save the whole world. But Mary was without sin in Her conception because God lives outside of time. Because of this, God could take the grace from the suffering of Jesus that saved the world (all people who ever lived and all people who ever would live) and through the Holy Spirit (God gives His gifts to humanity through the Holy Spirit) give it to Mary before She was born—and from that She was without sin.

Every human person after Adam and Eve was with sin, except for Mary. It was not because Mary was God (like Jesus was without sin because He was God). Mary was without sin because of Jesus. The purity of Mary has its source in the Cross. And so each woman must find her source of purity in the Cross as well.

Woman's Relationship with Jesus in the Eucharist

What kind of relationship does Jesus want with women in the Eucharist and on the Cross? During the time that a woman sits with Jesus, after she receives Him in the Eucharist, she wants to give Him love and to receive His Love. In living such a profound love relationship with Him, she is able to give Him great glory. A woman, in particular, can enter into such a deep love relationship with Jesus because of the great sensitivity of heart that she possesses. Her capacity for motherhood makes her finely attuned to 'others'. This enables her to enter easily into intimate relationships. And Jesus wants to use this gift of woman's to help her draw intimately close to Himself. When a husband and wife join in marital love, the husband gives himself, and the woman receives him and gives herself in return.

The first work of woman is to receive and then to give; to receive life and to give life; to receive that relationship with her husband and to give life from it. She receives her husband, gives herself to him in return, and then he gives himself to her again. That is a symbol of the sort of relationship that all of humanity should have with God. This is something very holy. God created husband and wife in such a way so that they could be a symbol to the world of how humanity should relate with Him. Women need to learn from this. Jesus comes to woman in the Eucharist. He makes Himself very weak, very little in bread so that she can take Him and break Him and eat Him. And because of that, because He is very humble, very little and very weak, she receives Him, and she wants to give all of herself to Him in return.

When a woman is with Jesus in the Eucharist she looks at the Heart of Jesus. She has the capability in a prophetic way to be attuned to how He feels and what He desires. She gives all of herself to Him. She receives His life into herself so that she can give that life to the world. The relationship which a woman has with Jesus in the Eucharist is the sort of relationship that a woman should have with people in the world. A woman should be greatly attuned to others, looking at their hearts and in turn give all of herself to serve them. Christ prays in the action of His sacrifice on the Cross. His body and soul are perfectly united in the prayer of fiat as He hands Himself over as an oblation for sin. And so, as a woman unites with Him—both in the Eucharist and in her daily Crosses accepted for Him—she must ask Him to pray in her. She must ask Him to make her life in union with His action prayer on the Cross, which in itself gives great glory to the Father.

When a woman sits with Jesus in the Eucharist she is in the midst of the most unfathomable Love. Jesus, the Man before her, knows how she feels, what she needs, how she works, and He gives all of Himself to her. His great gift of love to her naturally opens her. A woman naturally opens the deepest parts of herself in the presence of Love. A woman is like a sunflower which opens in the presence of the sun and turns towards it. In the same way, a woman opens in the presence of authentic love and follows it. The presence of such great love before her in Jesus' presence in the Eucharist—a love willing to give all in service and sacrifice to her—inspires a woman to open and receive such love, allowing it to transform her to imitate it.

Mary Rousseau refers to this communion with Jesus as such, "[In] this divine marital love...the Son of God makes Himself putty in the hands of sinners needing redemption...[and in] our acceptance of that gift...we make ourselves putty in the hands of Divine Love."[1] Jesus not

---

[1] *The Catholic Woman, Volume 3 – Wethersfield Institute Proceedings* (San Francisco: Ignatius Press, 1990), p. 20.

only fills a woman with His Love in the Eucharist, He transforms her—enhancing her already natural tendency of sensitivity to others and total self-gift—helping her to relate to the world in a way imitating His Own Heart.

In imitating the Love she has received from Jesus, a woman must look at others with her heart. She must notice how they feel and what they need and give all who they are to others. A woman learns in her relationship with Jesus, especially in the Eucharist, how to be humble like Jesus is humble—how to be weak and little like Jesus is weak and little. And this gift is not just to be weak and little for no reason, but to be weak and little so that she can be a gift that others receive and hold and do not fear. Through her little weakness in this way she calls forth other's love. She learns from Jesus how to give all of herself so that her husband will then learn from her how to give all himself and her children will learn from her how to give all themselves. By letting herself be captured by Jesus, she receives the strength she needs to let herself be captured by her husband, to be captured by the world. And by being a gift to her husband (and to the world), by receiving him into herself, she teaches him how to be a gift and to go out of himself.

Woman learns in prayer with Jesus, with His Heart in the Eucharist, how to give ALL like He does—even if someone will 'eat' her. When a woman is pregnant and gives birth to her child, that child eats from her. She is food. Jesus can help a woman learn to be selfless in this way. It is not only that she is physically food for her child. No, her feeding of her child from her breast is a sign that she always needs to be ready to give all—to be open and to give all to her children. It is a sign that she needs to never hold anything in her life for herself. She learns that through Jesus in the Eucharist because He gives Himself like food—and He gives all. He opens Himself totally and He allows for any person who wants to receive Him to come, which means He allows for any person who wants to come and wound Him to draw close.

If someone receives Jesus at Mass and has sin in his heart, or if someone does not pay attention to Him when he receives this gift of the Eucharist, or if one's mind wanders to think about unimportant things when he should be thanking and praising Jesus for His sacrificial Love, Jesus suffers great pain over such indifference. It is true that Jesus died, rose, and ascended into heaven. But it is also true that He mysteriously stays with humanity in the prison of the Eucharist. And He is present there as a Person. Can one fathom what it means for Jesus to make Himself bread? Can one begin to comprehend what it means for Jesus to sit for 2000 years giving all of Himself to people so that they can receive and wound Him? Although Jesus ascended into heaven, He still mysteriously continues to suffer from humanity's sin and indifference. And He does not suffer in a generic way—He suffers as a Man with a truly broken Heart.

When Jesus was on the Cross His Heart was pierced open—and it remains pierced open. That wound did not close. But Jesus does not complain, and He does not look at His Own wound. He looks at His Father in Heaven in obedient Love and trust and giving all of Himself. He looks at His children calling to them in Love to respond to His Love with the gift of themselves. When a woman prays with Jesus in the Eucharist, she can receive the grace she needs to do what Jesus did— to become a sacrifice of Love; to give herself like food not only to her children, but to the whole world; to remain open to receive people in Love and to allow them to touch her wounds so that she can love through those wounds.

Jesus in the Eucharist teaches a woman how to be a mother. He enters into a woman as a Child, to live in the womb of her heart. Mary shares her pregnancy with each woman in the Eucharist. Just like Mary treasured Jesus within her womb, a woman can treasure Jesus' Eucharistic presence within herself, within the womb of her heart. After Mary said 'Yes' to the angel and She received Jesus into Her womb, She immediately went to serve Her cousin Elizabeth in obedience. Each time a woman receives Jesus in the Eucharist, she is pregnant with Him. And this gift gives her all that she needs to imitate Mary and immediately go out and serve in obedience to the Father. The relationship that a woman can have with Jesus in the Eucharist is very deep, very special and very natural because He is a Man. In the Gospel of John Jesus said, *"I am the vine and you are the branches. Whoever remains in me will bear much fruit because without me you can do nothing."*[2] It is very important for a woman to live inside of Jesus. And He wants to live inside of each woman as well. This is possible through the Eucharist.

It is not easy for a woman to give all of herself. She is tired sometimes; other times, she simply may have no desire to serve or may be annoyed with the person she is serving. And in these times a woman may be tempted to think about herself and to withdraw from loving as Jesus calls her to do. It is not possible to be a woman like Jesus created her to be if she does not have grace from God. A woman receives this grace through her relationship with Jesus in the Eucharist to be as patient as He is, to forgive as He does, to love as He commanded her to do. Jesus can give this grace through means other than the

---

[2] John 15:5.

Eucharist—and He does give it to people who are not Catholic, but Catholics have been blessed with such a straight, direct, powerful path to this grace. A Catholic woman can receive His very Heart, which then can become her own. She receives Jesus and He opens her. He opens her so that she can give all. He gives her the strength to give all. He pulls her into His Own humility, His Own Faithfulness. Jesus did not sit in the Eucharist for 2000 years and then later became tired of it and simply leave. He stays and suffers. Whether someone receives Him with a lot of love, or if they receive Him as a joke, He gives Himself the same—He gives all. A woman must open herself and receive the depths of His passionate Love, and then strive to imitate it. St. Edith Stein said:

…When [a woman] has once realized that no one other than God is capable of *receiving* her completely for Himself and that it is sinful theft toward God to give oneself completely to one other than Him, then the surrender is no longer difficult and she becomes free of herself. Then it is also self-evident to her to enclose herself in her castle, whereas before, she was given to the storms which penetrated her from without again and again; and previously she had also gone into the world in order to seek something abroad which might be able to still her hunger. Now she has all that she needs; she reaches out when she is sent, and opens up only to that which may find admission to her. She is mistress of this castle as the handmaid of her Lord, and she is ready as handmaid for all whom the Lord desires her to serve. But, above all, this means that she is ready for him who was given to her as visible sovereign—for her spouse or, also, for those having authority over her in one way or other.[3]

It is very important that a woman has a deep relationship with Jesus in the Eucharist. She must ask Him to open her womanhood there. A woman needs love to open and to grow. When a woman feels attacked, her reaction is to close and to defend herself. But when a woman feels loved, her reaction is to open and to be calm, regardless of what difficulties she encounters. For example, in the natural world if a woman's husband loves her, it does not really matter to her how the rest of the world treats her. The security of his love makes others' rudeness (and even cruelty at times) unimportant and easily forgotten. One kiss from her husband in the evening can quickly erase an entire day's struggles.

In difficult situations a woman who knows she is beloved to someone can be calm and open to receive wounds from others and can still return love in the midst of suffering—for she has her source of love in her relationship with him. And so, if the security of human love can transform a woman in such a way, how much more powerful is the security of Divine Love, which can fill and surround a woman through her relationship with Jesus in the Eucharist? If a woman lives inside of Jesus, and she allows for Him to take her inside of Himself, she always will have Love around her, and she will not be afraid of anything. Jesus can open, fill, and transform a woman in such a way with His powerful Love. His Love can buffer any suffering she may encounter, and it can inspire her to heroically love difficult people.

---

[3] St. Edith Stein, *Woman,* Vol. 2, Second Ed., Revised, Eds. Lucy Gelber and Romaeus Leuven, O.C.D., Trans. By Freda Mary Oben (Washington D.C.: ICS Publications, 1987), p. 134.

Jesus wants to teach a woman her motherhood through the Eucharist. He, as a Child within her, teaches her how to be a mother. He wants to teach her how to be a wife through the Eucharist. He wants to teach her how to be a daughter—a daughter who always obeys her Father. A woman learns how to obey her Heavenly Father from Jesus in the Eucharist, Who also obeys His Father unto death on the Cross. Obedience took Him into the 'prison' (one could say) of bread and wine. He was God! He is God! He created everything. And He not only incarnated into a person, into a slave—but He then entered bread, because He did not want for anyone to fear to come to Him. If humanity saw Jesus in His glory, maybe people would fear or be embarrassed to go to Him or to speak to Him. But if a person sees Jesus as a lowly Servant of Love (an ordinary person from the street), he would not fear to go and speak with Him. Jesus wanted to become very low so that He could save all, everyone. A woman is to imitate Jesus in His humility in the Eucharist. She is to make herself simple, ordinary and low—a true servant of Love—so that none fear to come and receive God's Love from her. A woman can only come to truly be an icon of Jesus' servant Heart if she spends time resting with Him in His Eucharistic presence. By being with His presence in such a way, she is transformed. St. Edith Stein said:

To have divine love as its inner form, a woman's life must be a Eucharistic life. Only in a daily, confidential relationship with the Lord in the tabernacle can one forget self, become free of all one's own wishes and pretensions, and have a heart open to all the needs and wants of others. Whoever seeks to consult with the Eucharistic God in all her concerns, whoever lets herself be purified by the sanctifying power coming from the sacrifice at the altar, offering herself to the Lord in this sacrifice, whoever receives the Lord in her soul's innermost depth in Holy Communion cannot but be drawn ever more deeply and powerfully into the flow of divine life, incorporated into the Mystical Body of Christ, her heart converted to the likeness of the divine heart.[4]

A Woman's Relationship with Jesus on the Cross

"Standing by the Cross of Jesus were his mother and his mother's sister, Mary the wife of Clopas, and Mary of Magdala. When Jesus saw his mother and the disciple there whom he loved, he said to his mother, 'Woman, behold, your son.' Then he said to the disciple, 'Behold, your mother.' And from that hour the disciple took her into his home" (Jn 19:25-27). Jesus only said seven words or phrases while He was on the Cross. He was very quiet, and this is a very good example for women. Women can learn from Jesus to only speak when the Holy Spirit guides them to do so. These particular words about Mary and Jesus' relationship are very important. In the moment He spoke them, Jesus gave the possibility for healing all relationships between women and men.

The completion of such healing depends only on men and women themselves being open to receiving the gift of healing. Jesus took His greatest human treasure—the Heart of His Mother—and gave it to all of humanity. He knew that they would not love Her as they should. He knew that She would suffer in Her maternity. But He knew that She would obey. And because She was so close to Him, She would have the grace She needed from Her relationship with Jesus to give everything

---

[4] Stein, p. 55.

to everyone always. Jesus took man's wounded relationship with woman and healed it in the gift of His Mother. What happened with Adam and Eve? Adam should have protected Eve. Eve should have loved Adam. But it was not like that. And yet in this new relationship with His Mother that Jesus gave to humanity from the Cross, man and woman were again ordered to His Father's original plan.

When Jesus said to John, "You will be the son of My Mother," John was given the responsibility to protect Mary. Jesus said him, "Be her son. Live what it means to be a man." When a mother is older, her son always protects her and helps her. And so Jesus took Mary and entrusted her to John. Jesus also said to Mary, "Love him as your son." And Jesus not only gave John to Her, but He also gave each person in the world to be Her child. He said, "Love him like you love Me." Can one imagine how difficult that would be for Mary to do? She had a perfect Son—and She was supposed to give the same sort of love She had for Him to all people in the world, even to all sinners who so deeply hurt Him?

She stood under the Cross and when Jesus said, "Be his mother and the mother of all people," Mary had to love those people who crucified Jesus. She had to love them as if they were Jesus Himself. In Mary's Fiat to Her Son's command, one can see in Her an icon of the perfection of what God intended for a maternal Heart to be. That is the gift that Jesus gave to woman through the Cross: a possibility to be like Mary. For if each woman was given to Mary as a child, she was also given the possibility to become like Mary, for it is easy for a daughter to become like her mother. If a woman is the child of a perfect Mother, then she has the possibility to be a perfect mother like Mary. And Jesus gave that gift to woman on the Cross.

Another gift God gave to woman is the gift of receiving and giving life. Jesus teaches woman how to receive and give life on the Cross. He received eternal life and gave it to all of humanity on the Cross. And He asked His Mother, "Receive each person in the world to yourself as a son, as a daughter, and give them life, Mother." And how does Mary give life to her children? She takes them to Jesus on the Cross and resurrected. Every woman needs to be like Mary—to receive all persons God entrusts to her maternal care and to carry them to the Cross where they can find eternal life. From the Cross, Jesus began the Church—from His Heart on the Cross water and blood poured out birthing forth the Church. Jesus did not hold any part of Himself back but instead allowed that all that was inside of Him to pour forth so that people would have the possibility to receive eternal life and salvation. A woman needs to be that open—to allow all that is in her to pour forth in love for others.

After Jesus gave humanity Mary, Scripture says, *"Aware that everything was now finished, in order that the scripture might be fulfilled, Jesus said, 'I thirst.'" (Jn 19:28)* Why did Jesus say, "I thirst"? What did He want? Jesus was not only speaking about physical drink. If Jesus was almost dead and His job was to save the world He would not talk only about physical drink. Jesus thirsted for love. God wanted for each person to be full of His Love. But when sin entered the world, humanity lost the fullness of God's presence in their hearts. Something inside of the human heart was empty through sin, for sin had created in the human heart an empty place without life. This place empty of life thirsts for God, for God created humanity to always be full of His presence.

Jesus wanted to fill all hearts –to return the gift of God's fullness to the human heart—but people hardened by sin would not receive His drink of Love if they did not first feel the thirst frozen in their hearts. And so Jesus first had to give humanity a thirst, a thirst for heaven, a thirst for love, before He could quench it. Jesus had to suffer thirst to give humanity thirst so that He could then come and fill the human heart through His blood.

What a wondrous gift to have God thirst for a human's Love! And Jesus suffers a million times over from His fathomless love returned often by such human indifference. The human heart often forgets His fathomless Love, which is simply waiting to save. But Jesus never forgets. He sits continually in the Eucharist and gives, gives, gives, gives. The sacrifice of Mass is where a woman can meet with Jesus on the Cross. In each Mass she enters into His Cross. Each Mass is not a new sacrifice of the Cross—but, instead, in each Mass a woman can enter back into that one moment in time where Jesus dies to bring humanity salvation. God takes the human heart back into time in each Mass so that one can stand with Mary under the Cross. Jesus thirsts for a response of love there. And His love not only melts a woman's heart to feel her thirst again, but also heals a woman's heart so that she will be willing to suffer with Him in order to awaken thirst in others and in this carry them to Him.

The Healing of a Woman's Heart from the Cross

Why do you think Jesus gathered so many women to Himself on the Cross? Why were women especially attracted to Him and His Love pouring out for them from the Cross? It is because women were created to need a special kind of love, both from Jesus as God as well as from Jesus as Man and from all their brothers and sisters in humanity. And women found this love that they needed in its fullness in the expression of Jesus' Heart hung wide open pouring out all of His Love for each of them individually on the Cross. They found in Him the source of their hearts' healing from all the wounds caused by this lack of love in the world.

A woman's heart was created by the Father and Jesus—in the Holy Spirit, in Trinitarian Love—to be a heart especially full of sensitivity and in need of tenderness. This heart of woman is therefore easily broken open in the world by other's harshness or lack of sensitive love. A woman's heart has many little cracks and crevices that must be touched, opened, and filled with love; otherwise, she feels empty—for she was created to be opened and filled by God's Love through man. But men often ignore these sensitive places of a woman's heart, and they leave them untouched, unopened, and unfilled with love. Men do not understand a woman's heart because it is so different from their own. And so women are often hurt by this.

A woman's heart was created with a great need to trust, with a great need and dependence on others to help. A woman's heart was created with a natural openness, yet this openness and trust is often wounded by men who do not respect and meet this vulnerability with Love, but instead with judgment, impatience, or coldness. A woman's heart has been deeply wounded in this world by others' lack of care or response to her need, and so she has closed her heart and attempted to take control of her own life—she tries to erase the needs and vulnerability God Himself placed within her, out of fear of being hurt.

A woman's heart needs the fullness of Love to surround her in order to free her from fear of being herself. When love surrounds a woman, she is free to be open, vulnerable and sensitive; she is free to feel things deeply and to speak her heart in truth, for in such an atmosphere of love she finds the security she needs and surety that another will respond to her sensitive feelings with Love. Jesus was able on the Cross to meet with the deepest wounds of a woman's heart, for He was broken open in Love for her—He poured out the fullness of His life for her, to her, in her so that she had the secure atmosphere of love and trust that she needed to open fully to Him, to share her vulnerability and needs with Him, to share her sensitivity of heart with Him—and all of the wounds deep in her heart caused by others' neglect, insensitivity, or misunderstanding, and Jesus could heal all these parts of her femininity, of her being, with His healing Manly and Godly Love.

A woman has a deep need to be known and understood. She was created as a mystery to herself in many ways—she was given as a gift to man and to all of humanity (*"The Lord God said, 'It is not good for the man to be alone. I will make a suitable partner for him.' ... The Lord God then built up into a woman the rib that he had taken from the man. When he brought her to the man, the man said: 'This one, at last, is bone of my bones and flesh of my flesh;' That is why a man leaves his father and mother and clings to his wife, and the two of them become one body"* (Genesis 2:18, 22-23, 24). And she only becomes the fullness of that gift when she is opened, received, touched by man, by his love and need for her. She is made into herself when she can serve with the deepest part of her being simply by being open in need, trust, and love in the arms of he who loves her. She serves and becomes herself by guiding man back to himself through being beloved, by teaching man to love her delicately and strongly through needing this—calling this from his heart by her great vulnerability, trust, and need.

Her need for gentle love and courageous care awakens his need to love. By letting him touch her and open her and fill her—by allowing him to 'know her' with his body, mind, and heart—she helps him fulfill his vocation to love as well. A woman's heart was created with a deep need to be known and understood because a man's heart has a need to understand. They have union in this. A woman's heart has a need to trust and receive in love (even that which she does not understand and know) but a man's heart is created with a need and hunger to 'know'— to pour himself out fully and to enter a woman in order to know, to possess her. A man was created to possess woman by love—and a woman was created to be known and possessed by a man's love. It is all so mysteriously beautiful, but also logical—this original plan of the Father for humanity.

Yet, men and women fell in sin. Women were wounded and closed themselves. Men were wounded, for no one needed them to pour themselves out fully—no one trusted them to love, to possess her heart with love, and to guide. A man cannot read a book that is closed—and without reading, he does not grow in knowledge. In the same way, a man cannot 'read,' cannot come to 'know' in love, the heart of a woman if it is closed, and he cannot grow or pour out himself in love (grow in the knowledge of love) if no one allows him to. So, in this imperfect world wounded so deeply by sin, women must come to Jesus on the Cross. They must find the healing that their hearts' need in His Husbandly crucified gift of Love for them on the Cross. Only in this way will they have the healing and courage they need to remain open and vulnerable in trustful need love before men who inevitably will sometimes wound them by their indifference or neglect, in order to call men back to their original vocations of caring for another—of pouring himself out so fully in humble, patient, tender love that he enters the beloved deep enough to possess her.

This is the healing Jesus desires to give humanity through all women in the world. Men can find healing for their wounded hearts by coming to Jesus and striving to let Him love through them as fully as He did on the Cross. Men can find healing in striving to imitate Jesus. Yet, the fullness of their healing can only take place when women have the courage to be patient, forgiving, and open in vulnerable love so that men have a place to pour their life and love—into a woman's open, waiting heart. Please, my sisters, always remain open with Jesus. Trust His Love to be enough when your open, vulnerable heart is wounded. Receive the courage you need, from His Love possessing and dwelling within you, to always remain open and patient in fiat, being ready and willing to receive others love to yourself—even if waiting or receiving suffering instead wounds you. Your wounds will make you like Jesus, and united with Him, they will help the world.

A woman's heart was created with a need for a very unique, powerful and individual love. Such a love frees her to serve others with the fullness of God's Love. Jesus planted a special grace—a special flower of His Love—within the heart of every woman. Yet, she needs others' love of her in order to open and to allow this flower to grow freely and feed others. On the Cross He gave to all of humanity, but especially to women, the special kind of Love that their hearts hunger and yearn for. He gave them the total and absolute gift of Himself and devotion to their deepest needs. He made Himself patient—unto death—out of love for them. He was humble and loved them with a love that truly freed them to be themselves. They could trust Jesus—

crucified upon on the Cross, taking their sins and suffering unto Himself—to never hurt them.

Jesus' Love was so great on the Cross that He could go into the deepest wounds of their hearts and touch them, healing them with His Love. From the Cross, Jesus could touch their sensitive needs and fill them—make them complete in His Love. From the Cross, He reopens their womanhood and through His powerful Manly, Husbandly Love for them He frees them to dance in Love. Jesus is their security, their trust, their answer, their rest. He knows them. He desires to pour His life into them. He wants to possess them with His Love... Jesus only waits for them to receive Him and answer in return.

Look at how our Blessed Mother lived the fullness of what I teach to you today. Her heart was full of great need and sensitivity, yet She allowed Her heart to always dwell in God, Who provided Her with all. This love relationship She lived with Her God freed Her in Her womanhood and enabled Her to courageously stand open and vulnerable suffering with Jesus when so many men wounded Him and killed Him. She came to Him and remained with Him on the Cross, and through Her fiat Jesus was able to reach and heal many women in the world—throughout all time and history. Stand with Her at Jesus' Cross—enter the Cross with Him. If you simply live all Jesus has asked of you, that in itself is enough to deeply heal the world—a world wounded in masculinity and femininity, a world wounded deep in their hearts.

Woman and Prayer

A woman must use her femininity to relate to Jesus in prayer. She can relate to Him as child, trying to just 'be' with Him the way she would be with a child with whom she is pregnant. A woman can relate to Him as brother, listening to what He speaks about His life and telling Him about normal things in her day. What a woman needs is to form a real, living relationship with Jesus as a person. In relating to Jesus as spouse, a woman can pour out all of who she is into His arms and receive Him into herself. A woman may also pray differently depending on how old she is or where she is in life. When a woman is a little girl, she has one relationship with Jesus—she may think of God as a friend, as Someone Who can just be with her. She may relate to God as her Father. Later, when a girl is a teenager she may begin to relate with Jesus as a brother. But when a woman is an adult He can open a very deep relationship with her as a Child—Someone Who lives within her womb—as well as a very intimate relationship as a Husband. And that is a very deep love to share with Jesus—a Husband's Love.

If a woman is called to marriage and will have an earthly husband, she will be called to love Jesus inside of that man. Or if a woman is called to a consecrated life in some form, she will love Jesus as a Husband. But regardless of her particular vocation, every woman is called within her heart to an individual, spousal relationship with Jesus as her Husband. Every woman must fall in Love with Jesus. And this can be simply done by a woman by asking Him to make her fall in love with Him. Jesus has the key to each woman's heart—and He knows how to unlock for Himself the great torrents of Love contained within each woman's heart. Jesus can move and form a woman's heart in this way. Every woman should go to Mass and Adoration and ask Him for the gift of being in love with Him. Such a love will draw her into the most intimate relationship with Jesus as Spouse—living Spousal Love with Him in an inconceivably powerful way.

Women often have the special gift of faith which helps them to relate with God as a person. They must build on this natural gift and allow God to nurture it in their hearts so that in turn they can help nurture such a powerful relationship with God in other people's lives. A priest friend of mine once explained this as such:

Women have the gift of faith that men lack. (For example, on the day of the Resurrection the women have courageous, heroic faith. They were more able to believe in the Resurrection than the men. They also were strongest at the cross.) Who usually responds better, more openly, quickly, fully to God? Usually women. Why? When men listen, they listen to the content of what a person is saying. When women listen, they pay more attention to the person than the content. For example, there is a banker in France who always has his wife sit in the office with him when he has business meetings. After the meeting, the man knows the content of the conversation, the details of the business deal, etc., but he learns from his wife about the other businessman (like about his character, how he was feeling about the deal, whether he was telling the truth). This is because women see people with their hearts. They look to what is deepest in the other person. Men are rational and know reason and content, but women know the person and this is the more important aspect of communicating.

In faith, one must believe in something beyond understanding; one must believe because he trusts the Person of God. The content of what God reveals is beyond one's understanding. Men oftentimes try to reason out God's revelation, where women can just accept it (because they are

used to just accepting the person). Women say, "I don't understand, but I believe the Person of God." Faith is responding to a Person beyond understanding. This is why faith is easier for women. Women push forward in faith even when they don't understand, where men get stuck trying to reason the truth of a revelation.[5]

Although women may naturally have the gift of faith and prayer, it can still be quite hard in today's world for her to find the time she needs to use these gifts. There is no question that the present world is a 'Martha world.' What this means is that the world is very centered on 'doing;' it is very busy, and if a person is not willing to jump into the rushing current, she is often balked upon by those running about around her. And yet, there can be no argument that Jesus said in the Gospel, "*Mary has chosen the better part and it shall not be taken from her.*"[6] This is a passage that contemplative, cloistered sisters and hermits thrive on—for it is the meaning of their existence—to sit at the feet of Jesus in Love and to pray, listen, and simply 'be' with Him instead of 'do' for and with Him. Yet, Jesus was not only speaking to such special, chosen souls through these words to Martha. He was also speaking to each woman throughout all of time.

In this passage, Jesus was reminding woman that her first gift to man was that of *being* for him. *She* is a gift—not only what she can do or create—but *she* is a gift. Mary, in this story, is totally centered on Jesus. And Jesus desires every woman's heart to be like Mary's. How

---

[5] Fr. John Mary Foster, *Conference at the University of Notre Dame* (Notre Dame, Indiana: Fall, 1998).

[6] Luke 10:42.

in the world can this be possible in a 'Martha world'? The answer comes in the second part of Jesus' words here—for He gives a promise. He says, *"It shall not be taken from her."*[7] In these words Jesus is promising woman the grace she needs to keep the 'better part' chosen by Mary—which is a heart centered on Him in Love—regardless of what actions she may have to perform throughout the day.

Something key to living in such a way with Jesus is that every woman *stops* their running around from time to time and goes to sit at Jesus' feet—offering Him the gift of herself and simply resting in Love attentively listening to Him. And once a woman has taken such time with Him (each will need very different amounts of time to 'collect' with Him), then she can move about her day's activities remembering that her heart is filled to the brim with Jesus' presence and Love. And she should be careful to 'guard her heart' so that none of this gift spills out of her, but, instead, remains as a fountain flowing out of all she says, does, thinks, and speaks.

No one ever hears the end of this story in the Gospel. Perhaps after Jesus pointed Martha's mistake out to her, she may well have sat down next to Mary to listen to the teacher and rest in His presence. And perhaps after Jesus finished teaching, both of Mary and Martha got up and together finished preparing to serve. Jesus never said Martha's service was bad—He simply said that it was more important for a woman to sit and rest with Him in Love. He had to be the center of all her actions. When a woman's heart is resting in Jesus', then her service has very deep worth.

---

[7] Luke 10:42.

Practical tips on how a woman can keep a "Mary" heart in a "Martha" world

There is no one 'right' way to remain united with Jesus throughout the day. God created each woman differently, and He desires to meet with each human heart in a different way. The following are some suggestions I hope will guide the reader to a deeper relationship of Love with Jesus, which will flow over to all that she does. By no means is a person expected to follow all of these suggestions. I would suggest that the reader simply take from these suggestions the few that might truly 'strike' her heart and try to implement them slowly throughout her day. If something seems silly or impossible, then try a different one. I only pray that something here can help everyone.

-Be a docile baby resting in Jesus' arms—it is an attitude of heart. Keep your heart in state of rest; if Jesus allows you to be busy, fiat. It is great trust for you to just accept what He gives to you. If He allows you think of Him, fiat. If He allows you to sleep, fiat. Trust and surrender. Give Him your spiritual life and allow Him to arrange your day and your possibilities of meeting with Him in prayer as He desires. And each thing you do for your children, do for him. See Jesus in them.

–Ask yourself throughout the day, "How would Jesus speak in this situation? How would Jesus act?" Your relationship with Him should color all in your life.

-Think of being 'pregnant with him'—allow your heart to always be a 'resting place' for His presence and Love. Move slower in your day—like your heart filled to the brim with His Love—that you don't want to 'spill'. Sometimes, if you focus on doing everything one second slower—making a concerted effort, for example, to do everything as an act of love and in great peace—your day will become consumed with His presence, for you are meeting Him in Love in everything. (Open the door in peace, speak full of love, sit on the ground and look at a book with a child with Him, think of how united you are when you eat and how you are feeding His body—for you have gifted your body to Him in the act of receiving Him in the Eucharist, etc.)

-Sometimes less is more. Plan less, but do it slower, deeper, in peace and Love.

-Pursue simplicity.

-Instead of 'doing a lot' (being a mom and being a 'mom to the world' at the same time), offer your little doings with your children, etc., for others. Often women see so many needs in the world and they try to fill them all, and they lose their peace of heart and their relationship with Jesus in the meantime. But without Him, without listening to how He wants you to work, your actions for others have much less power and meaning. Realize that prayer is the most powerful way to change and help the entire world. Touch those who need you in your daily life and offer such little, ordinary acts of love for your children and those whom Jesus brings to you as a prayer for all those throughout the entire world that you would also want to help.

-In the morning before you get out of bed take 2 minutes to ask the Holy Spirit to consume and guide you; or do this while you make coffee. Put a sign that says, 'Holy Spirit,' and whisper a prayer while you make it. As you drink, think of drinking the Holy Spirit.

-Get in a habit each time you meet a frustration in the day to THANK Jesus for it—it is where He is meeting you from the Cross; Fast on His crucified Love, which means that you 'eat' all the little ways He allows you to share in His crosses with Him.

-Accept that you won't understand everything in your life— you are called to TRUST. Let LOVE be your guide…

-Rejoice when you feel lost and empty spiritually, when you are tired. This is how Jesus felt on the Cross. Don't change your life (like what you are doing)—if you are a mom, for example, you have to do all these things (caring for your children, laundry, cooking, shopping, etc.); just try to allow Jesus to slowly transform your reaction to your life, your relationship with what happens around you. Find Him in all and treasure His presence in your heart.

-Don't judge your own spiritual life. Don't even think about it… fiat. Find a good spiritual director or confessor, entrust your spiritual life to him, and then don't over-analyze yourself. If you have given yourself to Jesus, He is in control. Trust Him.

-Don't expect to see fruit from your spiritual life. Jesus did not see the fruit of His suffering while He hung on the Cross. Unite with Him there. Try to love Him and do what you think He desires for the sake of love itself—and not to see fruit. Entrust all fruit to Him and just be faithful.

-Seek greater silence of heart… turn off the TV, radio, computer and give Him a chance to speak (even if it is while you are driving in the car or making dinner).

-Make everything in your life a meeting with Jesus—every word you speak or don't speak; every step, every gesture.

Everything—sleep, work, rest, eating—all is done out of love in surrender to His will in order to receive His Love for the sake of His Love. Everything in your life speaks of Jesus' Love for you— and everything in your life speaks of Jesus' Love for the world through you. Watch and listen for Jesus' Love at every moment...

-Take and receive every situation that comes to you in joyful fiat, seeing in it Jesus' Kiss of Love (whether that situation be the Cross and suffering, or simple, childlike rest.) See the Beauty of His Love in all!!! This will give you joy in suffering."

-Seek a peaceful heart. If something breaks your peace, throw it away until later... don't think about it or deal with it then. If you keep peace, you have union with Jesus, and he will guide all.

-Because the Mass takes you back to the moment of His Crucifixion, as you live accepting God's will in each moment (especially when that will seems to 'crucify you'), you are living the Mass. Go deeper into the Mass in the Cross with Jesus. And may this focal point of your day move out and consume your whole life. May your whole life be living united to Jesus in the Mass. Maybe you cannot always go to Mass every day (depending on your state of life). But live then not from the Mass day to day, but Sunday to Sunday. Read the readings and take them literally as Jesus' answers to you (as if He were speaking to you) for that next week's work. Take all the suffering you endure and place it on the altar with Him—all of your work, all of your worry, all of your joy. If you focus on 'living the Mass,' your days will be anchored on that and it will be easier to keep union with Him. Live in Thanksgiving for the last Mass you attended and in preparation for the next. All day (all week) continually gather up in your heart everything that you want to place on the altar with Jesus as a sacrifice of Love. When you encounter sufferings and frustrations, be thankful that Jesus is allowing you to have something to offer Him; He is allowing you to live the Mass, suffer the Mass with Him during the week. And when you place those things on the altar with Him during the preparation of the gifts or Consecration, your life is transformed with the gifts into being a sacrifice of Love and you are transformed into being a living image of Jesus.

-In reading Jesus' words, He will fill your memory and consume your thoughts. This will help preserve you in Him. Read the Words He speaks in Scripture, and read His Heart and His Silence as well—read His Wounds and Suffering...Make time every day (or every week) to do this... really read and meditate on these things about your specific spiritual life with Jesus...

-Once a day think, "Jesus, how are *you* doing today? What can I do for *you*?"

-Just 'be with Him' while you do everything. You can have union with Him in prayer, silence, or reading, but you can also have union with Him in desire and suffering 'no union'... When you want to have more time to be with Him and you simply cannot have it (because your baby is sick or your sister is in the hospital), unite with Him in your desire. He also desired union with His Father on the Cross, and yet He felt far and abandoned.

-Surrender to all He has given to you; Fiat to all He has placed in your life in the present; and Fiat to all His plans for your life to come. This, His Love praying 'Fiat' in you, should be your constant prayer, as well as your constant drink. When you pray fiat, you allow for His blood to flow in you, through you. When you say fiat, you allow not only His Heart's Love, but its being in entirety, to physically beat living within you. In your Fiat, you allow His presence to draw ever so close to you, to open and fill you deep, full, and wide with the very source and essence of His Love. In this you are present to Him on the Cross as well, for you live dwelling in Him and He in you. Just live your wifely duty, motherly duty, sisterly duty, etc. But live it with Him, for Him, in Him.

··

To think about:

1. What are the deepest wounds from your life that you can bring to Jesus to heal on the Cross?
2. How can your life be more Eucharistic?
   a. Who is Jesus to you?
   b. Who do you want Him to be?
3. What is your first memory of God? Why is that important to you?
4. What is your favorite way to pray? Somehow find time to pray this way!
5. What does it mean to be 'pregnant' with Jesus' Heart? How should that change the way you live?
6. Do think like Jesus? Feel like Jesus? Remember like Jesus? Speak like Jesus? Pray like Jesus? Act like Jesus? Love like Jesus? Where can you grow? Ask Jesus in what area He wants to perfect your love to be more like His own—He will somehow show you....

7. What does it mean to 'fiat' (to surrender to God's will like Mary did in the Annunciation)?

Chapter 9

The Ideal of the Saints
and Our Lady as God's Masterpiece of Femininity

"Be who God meant you to be and you will set the world on fire!" said Saint Catherine of Siena. And so it is of the greatest importance that women understand and become who God made them to be—not only for themselves to be fulfilled and find happiness, but also *for the world* that they will influence by the fire of love within themselves. "Be who you are!" a priest used to tell me—and it is precisely by allowing God and His Love to transform a person into *His* great ideal of her identity that one can most powerfully impact the world. It is by *'being'* who God wants and by living radical, heroic love that a woman will transform society much more than any words she could say or works she could perform. The saints lived this heroic ideal to the upmost degree, and so we should look to them as shining examples of practically how a woman can live out her vocation to holiness. Yes, more than to a function in this world, a woman's first vocation is one of simply living holiness in itself in both big and little things day in and day out and by simply *being* a gift of love.

How did the saints live their vocations of womanhood? How were they a gift, a helpmate, mothers, pure, and prayerful? I could write an entire book on how each one embraced each of the chapters written in this book. Instead, I would like to simply give an overview of a few examples of each of these characteristics, and then turn our gaze to Our Lady, the Queen of all Saints.

The lives of the saints are full of examples of holiness being lived out through womanhood. In Scripture, we see that St. Elizabeth was so attuned to the Holy Spirit that she was enlightened about Our Lady's pregnancy, and she was not jealous of the work that God was doing in her little Cousin's life, but was rather filled with gratitude, praise, and adoration of His great work and goodness. Ruth in the Old Testament lived a deep friendship with Naomi her mother-in-law. She was a faithful daughter-in-law who refused to abandon her aging mother-in-law in times of trouble. Suzanna held purity in such esteem that she was willing to go on trial in order to be faithful to God—and God saw her in her lowliness, trust, and purity of heart and rescued her. Ester acted like a mother to the entire Jewish population when she went before the king to beg for their lives. It said that she wholeheartedly trusted in the Lord, and He heard her prayer. Judith as well was a strong mama and leader of her people—cultivating in their hearts a great faith by encouraging them to trust in God, as well as by delivering them from evil. The women of the New Testament were great helpmates in Jesus' work. Peter's mother-in-law got up and served Jesus as soon as she was healed. Mary and Martha often provided hospitality for Jesus and the disciples. St. Mary Magdalene stood faithful, with Our Lady, under the Cross and spent the rest of her life after Jesus' Ascension devoted to prayer in a cave. Many women, in fact, followed the Lord helping to serve in His work and remaining faithful in suffering prayer and love under the Cross. Yet, there are also the great virtues that we see in the lives of Sarah, Rebecca, Rachel, Leah, Moses' mother who treasured his life and saved him from death, and that we see in the lives of the mother of the Maccabees and Sarah in the book of Tobit.

The life of the Church for 2000 years has been full of brilliant examples of courage, faithfulness, purity, humility, generosity, patience, love, and holiness. St. Catherine of Sienna humbly served her parents, served the poor, and then served the Pope. St. Katherine Drexel was a great mother of souls. Neither race nor economic class mattered to her when she met a child or family in need. She spent her entire life pouring herself out for children—setting up schools and being the presence of a mother. St. Cecilia, St. Lucy, St. Agatha, St. Dymphna, and St. Agnes were all young girls who radiated purity to such a great degree that in their choosing purity and Jesus even over and unto death, those around them were forced to lift their eyes up to God. St. Clare of Assisi was a helpmate to St. Francis and his brothers simply by upholding them in prayer. St. Gianna Molla was so strong in her vocation of motherhood—to the call of her heart to receive, nurture and give life—that she sacrificed her very own life to save her unborn child. St. Rose of Lima had such a spirit of peace that when her city was invaded by those wanting to destroy the churches, the people ran to her for protection, and she saved them just by praying. St. Teresa of Avila was a teacher of souls and St. Therese of Lisieux nurtured the interior life of her novices. St. Kateri Tekhawitha gave up everything for her 'pearl of great price'—leaving both her family and her Indian people in order to follow the God of Jesus with Whom she had fallen in love. St. Faustina and St. Margaret Mary Alacoque taught people how to love Jesus—all about His Love and what His Love desired. They were spiritual masters of the Heart of Jesus, but didn't keep that for themselves—instead, they nursed their children with Christ's teachings of charity. St. Bridget of Sweden, St. Monica, St. Elizabeth of Hungry, and St. Rita were all holy mothers devoted to the salvation of their husbands and children—willing to lose everything in order to save their souls. St. Mother Teresa spent her entire lifetime being the helpmate of humanity and a great mother to people both in body and soul. St. Josephine Bakhita lived forgiveness to the greatest degree possible, even thanking the Lord for her enslavement since it eventually led her to Christ and to be His bride. And as we already spoke about—St. Maria Goretti so treasured purity that she would rather have died than to allow her purity to be violated. All of these women encompassed what is written in Proverbs about a virtuous woman.

Proverbs 31:10-31 lists a whole series of virtuous qualities attributed to a holy wife. As we have reflected on womanhood, we see how all women are called to embrace these characteristics—whether they be married, consecrated, or single. Each woman, regardless of her vocation, is called to live as part of the Church, which is the Bride of Christ. Each soul is called to live a spousal relationship with God, which then can be practically lived out in the various vocations. By literally considering herself a 'wife of Christ' bound to fulfill such duties as described in Proverbs in her mystical marriage, a woman can greatly enrich her spousal relationship with Him. Here in Scripture the same word for 'wife' (or 'woman') in Hebrew and Latin is used as is used in Genesis when woman is created from man, and he clings to her as 'wife'—naked, but without shame. This describes how woman was originally created to be. We can clearly see the saints in this description of the virtuous woman. And through this passage, we can be deeply connected to a woman's relationship with Jesus on the Cross and in the Eucharist. Proverbs states:

"When one finds a worthy wife, her value is far beyond pearls.
(Her value is beyond that of the beauty of a wedding day.)
Her husband, entrusting his heart to her, has an unfailing prize.
(Christ entrusts His very Heart to each of us—and collectively the
Church—in the Eucharist and on the Cross.)
She brings him good, and not evil, all the days of her life.
She obtains wool and flax and makes cloth with skillful hands.
Like merchant ships, she secures her provisions from afar.
She rises while it is still night, and distributes food to her household.
She picks out a field to purchase; out of her earnings she plants a
vineyard.
(She does all this 'at night'—in secret and in the silence, hiddenness
and darkness of the Cross. She is active in serving Him—
feeding the world—'her household'—from what He has shared
with her).
She is girt about with strength, and sturdy are her arms (Her arms
are 'outstretched' in service, as well as with her Husband's on
the Cross.)
She enjoys the success of her dealings; at night her lamp is
undimmed.
(She is stable and faithful—she is the 'Woman' under the Cross—
'clothed with the sun'—who through her union with Jesus
'succeeds' in crushing satan together with Our Lady.)
She puts her hands to the distaff, and her fingers ply the spindle.
She reaches out her hands to the poor, and extends her arms to the
needy.

She fears not the snow for her household; all her charges are doubly clothed.

She makes her own coverlets; fine linen and purple are her clothing.

(She toils and labors with her Husband to provide for the poor, the needy—and she trusts Him to provide for her. She gives forth life from what she receives.)

Her husband is prominent at the city gates as he sits with the elders of the land.

(The crucified Husband—hanging as 'King' at the gates of the city—rejected by the elders—but prominent by the election of the Father.)

She makes garments and sells them, and stocks the merchants with belts.

She is clothed with strength and dignity, and she laughs at the days to come.

She opens her mouth in wisdom, and on her tongue is kindly counsel.

She watches the conduct of her household, and eats not her food in idleness.

Her children rise up and praise her; her husband, too, extols her:

Many are the women of proven worth, but you have excelled them all."

(This all comes from her deep, daily union with her Husband Jesus).

Charm is deceptive and beauty fleeting; the woman who fears the LORD is to be praised.

Give her a reward of her labors, and let her works praise her at the city gates."

Sirach 26:1-4, 13-18 has a similar strength when reflected on in light of the vocation of woman—especially one who strives to live virtuously and in union with Christ:

> *"Happy the husband of a good wife, twice-lengthened are his days;*
> *A worthy wife brings joy to her husband, peaceful and full is his*
> *life. A good wife is a generous gift bestowed upon him who fears*
> *the LORD; Be he rich or poor, his heart is content, and a smile*
> *is ever on his face...*

> (This speaks of how a holy woman can bring consolation to Jesus—poor and suffering on the Cross—through letting Him 'cling to her' as wife even in His sweaty, bloody, crucified pain. When He sees His a soul love Him fully, generously, surrendered—it gives His Heart a 'smile'—even if it is crucified.)

> *A gracious wife delights her husband, her thoughtfulness puts flesh*
> *on his bones;*

> (As a saintly woman willingly unites with her crucified Husband in pain, she makes up what is lacking in His strength. (Col 1:24) She is part of Him, so she must also 'suffer her part'— and in doing that she helps Him enflesh His Love in the world.)

> *A gift from the LORD is her governed speech, and her firm virtue is*
> *of surpassing worth.*

> (This speaks of the prophetic vocation of a consecrated woman— echoing Pope Benedict's words to consecrated religious on May 8th, 2007: *"Only **union with God** can cause and strengthen the 'prophetic' role of your mission, which consists in the 'proclamation of the heavenly kingdom,' an indispensable*

proclamation in every age and society.")

Choicest of blessings is a modest wife, priceless her chaste person.

(This speaks of a woman's call to live out the original virginal value
   of woman.)

Like the sun rising in the LORD'S heavens, the beauty of a virtuous
   wife is the radiance of her home. Like the light which shines
   above the holy lampstand, are her beauty of face and graceful
   figure. Golden columns on silver bases are her shapely limbs and
   steady feet."

(This clearly reflects Mary in Revelation 12:1—'the 'woman'
   (Greek: gune = 'woman'/'wife') clothed with the Sun...'—a light
   shining from Her union with both her 'Son' and her 'Spouse.')

Let us pray that we may enflesh what is written in Scripture about
a virtuous woman. And may the saints' examples and intercession
both inspire us and gain us the grace we need to live our vocations as
heroically as they did!

Our Lady—the Queen of all Saints and God's Masterpiece of Femininity

More than all else, we must at the end look to Our Holy Mother in
Heaven. She is the Ideal Masterpiece of Femininity. Archbishop
Fulton Sheen writes about her in his book, *The World's First Love:*

"Everyone is in love with an ideal love. We all love something more
than we love. When that overflow ceases, love stops. That ideal love
we see beyond all creature-love, to which we instinctively turn when
flesh-love fails, is the same ideal that God had in His Heart from all

eternity—the Lady whom He calls 'Mother.' She is the one whom every man loves when he loves a woman—whether he knows it or not. She is what woman wants to be when she looks at herself. She is the woman whom every man marries in ideal when he takes a spouse, she is hidden as an ideal in the discontent of every woman with the carnal aggressiveness of man; she is the secret desire every woman has to be honored and fostered; she is the way every woman wants to command respect and love because of the beauty of her goodness of body and soul. And this blueprint love, whom God loved before the world was made, this Dream Woman before women were, is the one of whom every heart can say in its depth of depths: 'She is the woman I love!'" (pp. 9-10)

One characteristic that strikes me so brilliantly about Our Lady's holiness is Her bold humility. She truly is the humblest of God's creatures. St. Catherine of Siena used to say that humility is knowing that 'God is God and I am not.' Who personified such humility more greatly than Our Lady? When God sent an angel to Her to ask about being the Mother of God, She obediently and immediately consented in trust, and yet She did not look at Herself in the matter. The gaze of Her Heart was immediately drawn to heaven, and Scripture records the hymn of praise and love that She sang to God in the Magnificat. To the degree that one is humble—empty of herself and open to God— God can fill her soul with His Own Divine Life and Love. Our Lady was consumed by this Life and Love as the Holy Spirit not only overshadowed Her exteriorly in the Annunciation, but intimately united to what was physically and spiritually most interior within Her in order to form the little Body of Baby Jesus.

In this Mary, perfectly exemplifies what we discussed about a woman being a mystery, for She truly was the 'garden enclosed' spoken of in the Song of Songs. Her Heart was a secret garden where the Lord came to find rest and do the most marvelous work He had ever done—the work of creating and giving to us a Savior Who would redeem us. Our Lady—the Immaculate Conception and Her Most Immaculate Heart—was perfect purity, which means that She was the perfect tabernacle of Our Lord. She was the spotless, unblemished Bride of the Song of Songs who was able to reflect all of the refulgence of God's Life, Love, and Holiness. She was full of God—totally His—in mind, body, heart, and soul. Nothing separated Her Immaculate Heart from union with His Own. Her Heartbeat was like His—in perfect union with each other. St. Thomas Aquinas wrote about how we become what we love—when two friends share a friendship a mutual compenetration of hearts takes place. In the end, it feels as if they shared one heart in two bodies. This is how Mary lived with Jesus. Her purity was complete with His.

In all of this, Our Lady was God's gift 'par-excellence'. She was a gift to Himself, to Her parents Anna and Joachim, to Joseph and Jesus, to the Apostles and disciples, and to all of us. She was a perfect gift. What God conceived of Her in His Mind She was in reality. She was sinless. She always did His will. Her Body was possessed by Him to such a degree that His Son took root in Her Flesh. Her Mind was filled with His Word. Her Spirit was filled with His Holy Spirit. Her Soul was a transparent tabernacle of His Divine Love.

Mary was God's Helpmate 'par-excellence.' She was the Father's Helpmate in providing a place for His Spirit to possess so fully that Jesus became incarnate and was given to the world from Her Body and

Heart. She was humanity's helpmate in that she gave them a Redeemer. She was Jesus' Helpmate under the Cross:

> "St. Albert the Great says that the Blessed Virgin was not chosen by the Lord to be a minister, but to be a spouse and help, after the words of Genesis: 'Let us make for Him a helpmate like unto himself." (Gen 11:18) The Most Holy Virgin is not a Vicar, (that is to say an instrument), but a coadjutor and a **companion** participating in the reign as she participated in the Passion... the wounds that Christ received in His Body, she felt in Her Heart.[1]
>
> "What then is the Role of Mary in the Passion? Nothing more than that of a help to Christ, 'a help like unto Himself' as St. Albert the Great says. For Mary is not formally a Priest on Calvary, but only the Associate of the Sovereign Priest. It is by her union of charity with Christ that she collaborated in the Redemption, it is by her Immaculate Heart that she is our Mother, as it is by His Sacred Heart that Jesus brought us into life.
>
> Jesus told St Bridget, "Her Heart was in My Heart and that is why I can say that My Mother and I have saved mankind as with one Heart, I by suffering in My heart and My Flesh, and she by the sorrow of the heart and for love."[2]
>
> His is a sacrifice that in the burning fire of suffering consumes within itself the entire godforsakenness of the sinner—and thus it is not only the cost physically but also the most spiritually agonizing sacrifice of all. What, then, is Mary's position now in relation to this

---

[1] Paul Phillippe, O.P., *The Blessed Virgin and the Priesthood* (Chicago: Henry Regnery Company, 1955), p. 36.

[2] Phillippe, p. 61.

*divine and human sacrifice?... **She embraces it with him, since she does not revoke her Yes (fiat) but remains faithful to it to the last. <u>She lets it be done</u>.** She offers to the Father, as she always has done, this self-sacrificing, sacrificial Victim, but in such a way that this offering (oblatio) is for her the most heartrending renunciation, only thereby making her oblation truly into a sacrifice, the surrender of what is dearest of all. How much sooner would the Mother suffer in the place of her Son all that he has to undergo! How terrible it is to have to assent to this sacrifice, which, from a worldly perspective, is the most meaningless and hopeless of all!** And when in Holy Mass, during the Canon, the Church again and again speaks of a sacrifice offered and recalls that it is not only the sacrifice of the Son that is commemorated but that the Church herself fully participates in the act of sacrifice, where else has she truly realized what this her offering to the Father of the Son, costs her except at that moment when, in Mary, she offered up her Son to the Father? Sinners in the Church cannot in fact realize this; they must be glad, rather, that Christ offers himself for them. And the Church does not exist except in real subjects.* **Alone, this all-holy woman, and at most just a few others who have been purified to the point of purest love, can gauge what sword it is that pierces the heart of the Church when she for her part sacrifices to the Father this self-sacrificing Lamb."[3]**

Our Lady was a Mother 'par-excellence'—and still remains Our

---

[3] Hans Urs Von Balthasar, *Priestly Spirituality* (San Francisco: Ignatius Press, 2013), p. 49.

Mother from Heaven. The entire purpose of Her life was to receive, protect, nurture and give Jesus—Who *is* our life—to all souls who come to Her asking Her intercession. Under the Cross in a special way Jesus gave Her to us when He entrusted Her to St. John. In saying, *"Woman, behold your son... Son, behold your Mother..."* Jesus was speaking to each one of us. If we are the Body of Christ, She cares for us (Her Son's Body) to the same degree that She cared for His physical Body as a child. And as a spiritual Mother, She nurses us at the breast of Divine Wisdom through the Holy Spirit, Who penetrates every part of Her being. She teaches us by example and word how to surrender fully to the torrent of God's Love. She is truly Our Mom.

The Blessed Mother is the one soul who always listened to the will of God and fulfilled it. And so, She wants to help each soul discerning her vocation—her call by God. She is a great 'saint maker' who, like a good Mother, makes sure that our ears are clear and hands are free from the world in order to hear the Voice of God and respond fully in 'Fiat' as She did. Every moment of Her Life—especially from the Annunciation unto Her Death—Her Heart beat 'Fiat'—'Thy will be done, Lord.' She can help us to 'Fiat' as well, as a good mother holds the hands of her child teaching them to walk. And She prays with us and for us. She loves God and so She loves us because of His Love for us. She desires His will for our lives because She wants Him to be glorified in us. She is full of the Spirit and shares that Spirit with us— as the Mediatrix of all Graces.

And Our Lady is our model in everything we reflected on in a woman's relationship to Jesus in prayer, under the Cross and in the Eucharist. Being the first tabernacle and spending many nights adoring Jesus in Her arms, She can best teach us how to love Him

Eucharistically. Having spent 33 years praying with Him—God Incarnate—She can teach us His secrets of prayer. And having stood—enduring the darkest of pain—with Jesus under the Cross, She can best aid us in carrying our own crosses and in keeping hope in our hearts when this world presses too heavily upon us. There are endless mysteries to be learned from Mother Mary's life and love because it was God's Life and Love that possessed Her at all times—and God is infinite. I pray that She may hold each of us reading this retreat close to Her Immaculate Heart and that through our contact with Her (Whose Heart is a 'window' into Heaven—for God lives in Her) we, too, may learn to be united as one with Jesus both here on earth and forever in eternity.

Totus Tuus ego sum Maria.
I am all yours, Mary.
Et Omnia mea tua sunt.
And all that I have is yours.
Accipio me in tua presencia.
Accept me into your presence.
Praebe mihi cor tuum.
Give me your heart.

(Prayer by St. Pope John Paul II)

∎∎ı

To think about:

1. How does God want to make me a saint by using my femininity?
2. Which women saints am I attracted to or most greatly desire to imitate and why?
3. What heroic virtue(s) is God asking me to live in my life?
4. Which Scriptures speak most profoundly to me of God's call to women?
5. Which women of the Bible do I see as the best examples of how I am called to live feminine holiness?
6. What attributes of Mary do I most admire and how can I imitate them?
7. What can I do every day to step by step draw closer to Our Lady and imitate her holiness?

The History of this Book

In 1997, I found myself sitting on the floor of a large room off the main section of one of the floors of the University of Notre Dame Library. The room was being used for the Jacques Maritain Center— which was at the time headed up by Professor Ralph McInerny. This internationally renowned and respected scholar, author, lecturer, philosopher, and theologian specialized in the works of St. Thomas Aquinas and the Documents of Vatican II. At the time, I was studying as an undergraduate in the Theology Department, and I was trying to very carefully pick and choose the best of the best courses that Notre Dame had to offer. This often included my taking graduate courses, as well as directed reading courses individually with the expert professors whose theology was crystal clear.

Professor McInerny was at the top of my list, and so I quickly sought out permission to have his philosophy classes count as theology credits, and I made an appointment with him to ask if he would individually do a directed readings course with me. He was an expert on Vatican II, and I thought maybe we could read the documents and he could guide me. Of course, being generous of heart, he immediately agreed. Word spread among the students and our directed readings course turned into a 30-person class, as people requested to join us. We met on Wednesday evenings for several hours as he sat in a chair and we all sat on the floor at his feet discussing Vatican II. At the end of the semester, he told us each to pick a topic and to write a 20-page paper on it. I chose the Vocation of Women in light of Vatican II. Professor McInerny loved my paper and asked me if he could publish part of it in one of the magazines that he edited. He encouraged me to pursue studying, writing, and speaking on this topic.

In 2003, I found myself tucked away in Kansk, Siberia. The priest assigned to the small parish there asked me if I would lead a several day retreat for the women on the vocation of women. I didn't have my paper from Notre Dame available, but I prayed and came up with several conferences—most of which covered the topics in each of the chapters of this book. At Notre Dame, I was writing for the well-educated and arguing with theologians about God's true gift of femininity. I struggled greatly during the four years I was at Notre Dame with various professors' false ideas of feminism. What I wrote there was to inspire a **holy feminism to enlighten and combat the evil feminism.** But in the retreat I was to give tucked away in Russia, I would be speaking to the uneducated, very simple-hearted peasants of the Russian tundra. What I discovered was that the truths that I wanted to explain in both situations were the same, I simply had to readjust my language depending on my audience (and according to my very simple and basic Russian vocabulary).

When I came home from the missions at the end of the summer of 2006, my sister Lisa was lamenting the lack of spiritual food available for women, especially a simple, American wife and mom. I offered to give her a retreat at her house every evening for a week based on my work for Professor McInerny and the retreat I had given in Russia. She was so thankful. I added to my work some new material that I had found reading Pope John Paul II's *Theology of the Body*, which I had been able to acquire in both English and the Holy Father's original

Polish. This was before this work had become as popular as it is today. Lisa was thrilled by what the Holy Spirit did between us that week and she asked if I would be willing to do such a retreat for other women. And so we hosted our first Women's Retreat at my parents' house over several evenings, and it was very well attended.

Lastly, my Polish friends heard about my work with the Vocation of Women. Some priests in Poland contacted me and said that they were having a week-long retreat on the Vocation of Women and Men. A Franciscan priest would be able to speak to the men for a couple of days, but they asked if I could do the sections on the vocation of women (and in the end they asked me to add one last conference with my prayerful considerations about the vocation of men as well).

This book in your hands right now is the fruit of both my original paper for Professor McInerny, as well as the retreats that I led on this topic. I hope and pray that Our Lady and Her Son are able to touch your hearts deeply through what is presented here.

Testimonials

"I picked this book up and could not put it down until I turned the final page... and I'm a man! If it captivated me to such a degree, I can only marvel at the wondrous effect it will have on women! This book is so uniquely beautiful that I would not be at all surprised if in time it is recognized as a classic in Catholic women's literature. I would encourage every woman to read this treatise and to hold on to it for her entire life... keep returning to it; and finally... leave it as a special heirloom to someone you love dearly." – **Lawrence Edward Tucker, SOLT, author of** *The Redemption of San Isidro; To Whom The Heart Decided To Love; Adventures In The Father's Joy; The Prayer of Jesus Crucified (La Oracion de Jesus Crucificado);* **and the new Catholic music album/CD,** *So Shine* **by brothersister**

"Mary Kloska takes on an important, though much neglected issue: the real differences between women and men, with a focus on the impact of those differences on women's spirituality. The joy of reading this is that in place of the anger that sometimes accompanies such issues, Mary gently and calmly observes the differences and celebrates both, even as she focuses her attention on the spiritual gifts of women. I, a man, have directed women, and I know a number of women who give spiritual direction to men, yet Mary's insights into the spiritual life of women offer far more insight than I can. In addition, her experience comes from her having lived on four continents, among very diverse people — North America, Europe, Africa and Asia, which gives her insights breadth. Her own spiritual life is the obvious source of her depth. Her book is a profound aid in a woman's spiritual development." – **Fr. Mitch Pacwa, SJ, president and founder of Ignatius Productions and senior fellow of the St. Paul Center for Biblical Theology**

"What a beautiful retreat for women! I love it. Full of deep insights. I can assure you from reading the book …that it is full of joy and peace and that it actually helped me at age 82 (even though I wrote a whole book about women and several books that I use on retreats myself). I still found new insights in this book. So even if you have been to women's retreats, this could give you something new and very important." – **Dr. Ronda Chervin, leader of dozens of women's retreats, and author of** *Feminine, Free, and Faithful*

"*The Holiness of Womanhood* contains much wisdom and Truth for any woman who really wants to become what God created her to be. Having lived through the rise of women's liberation in the sixties and seventies, which began the release of tons of literature about women that only polluted the mind, I find this book refreshing. It gives a Godly spin to femininity and has many riches for any woman who wants to be a woman of God." – **Clare R. Ten Eyck, Ed.D., Catholic Therapist and Retreat Director**

"Mary Kloska's retreat for women, especially in their early twenties, lays out the principles for motivating a young person's true identity in the making. Even more, a mother of a family can find in this book, easy to read and think about, practical insights to help her daughters mature toward a deep sense of potential motherhood. Then she can more truly discern an authentic spouse to love her and her children in marriage with sacrificial love." – *Fr. Basil Cole, Professor of moral, spiritual, and dogmatic theology at the Dominican House of Studies*

"This book provides a much needed insight into authentic femininity, and is a must read for young and old women alike, who wish to delve deeper into their individual vocations and their meaning and purpose as a daughter of the King." – **Theresa A. Thomas, Mother of six daughters, 15-year family columnist at "Today's Catholic News," contributor to Integrated Catholic Life website, Catholic Exchange, freelance writer and author of *Big Hearted: Inspiring Stories from Every Day Families* (Scepter, 2013)**

Made in the USA
Monee, IL
12 April 2023

31594196R00125